BEATING the Used-Car HUSTLE

By Robert Levering

With Photographs by Janet Fries

Chronicle Books/San Francisco

Cover photo of Bob White of "Beautiful" Bob's Auto Sales, San Francisco, by Janet Fries.

Printed in the United States of America.

Library of Congress Cataloging in Publication Data

Levering, Robert, 1944-
Beating the used-car hustle.

Bibliography: p.
1. Used car trade — United States. 2. Automobiles — Purchasing. — I. Title.
HD9710.U52L48 629.22'22 79-18647
ISBN 0-87701-150-8

Book and cover design by Brenn Lea Pearson.
Composition by Hansen & Associates.

Chronicle Books
870 Market Street
San Francisco, CA 94102

Contents

CONTENTS

1 PSYCHING into the used car game

This book should be dedicated to Bernie, a young, slickly dressed, fast-talking car salesman.

Bernie pulled a "bait-and-switch" routine on me. I did not know what that term meant when we met more than a year ago. But I knew then that I felt like punching Bernie in the nose.

You see, Bernie tricked me into making a half-hour-long drive to his car lot. I had called all the Dodge dealers in the area to find out if any had used four-door Dodge Colts in stock. I had already struck out with five phone calls when I dialed Bernie's car dealership.

"Sure. We've got a half dozen of them here on the floor right now," Bernie replied to my inquiry. "Come right on down."

After several weeks of frustrated used car hunting, I was willing to go almost anywhere to see a selection of the kind of car I wanted to buy. So I jumped into my trusty '65 Dodge Dart and caught the freeway south.

No sooner had Bernie introduced himself to me at his lot than he flashed a smarmy smile at me and said, "I lied to you on the telephone, Bob. We don't have any used Colts right now. But I can put you into a brand new Colt for less than $4,000 – which isn't much more expensive than buying a recent model second-hand one."

Perhaps I would not have written this book if my car had not run out of gas on the freeway as I returned home after my extremely brief encounter with Bernie. (Among other reasons I wanted to get rid of the Dart was the fact that its fuel gauge didn't register.) But Bernie's cute little trick was only the final straw after several weeks of similar confrontations with his breed of hustler.

Being at the mercy of unscrupulous creeps like Bernie wasn't the only part of buying a used car that annoyed me. I didn't understand much about how to go about picking a model, where to buy one, how to avoid buying a lemon, or how to finance a car. I had bought every other car I had owned (several VW Beetles, an old Buick LaSabre, and the Dart) from relatives, friends, or acquaintances. I knew enough about cars to be a decent backyard mechanic and do my own oil changes, lubes, tune-ups, brake jobs, and even once put in a new clutch.

But buying a dependable used car from a stranger was an entirely different matter. I could tell it was an elaborate game – one whose rules were entirely foreign to me. I suspected that the game is equally strange to most consumers – one of life's experiences to be endured with your eyes closed and hands clasped in hopes that with some luck you won't lose all your money in the process.

After meeting Bernie, I vowed to learn everything I could about buying a used car. I fully expected to be driving used cars for the rest of my life, considering the impact of inflation on the price of new cars. What's more, a car is likely to be one of my biggest single investments, and my car expenses have always chewed up sizable chunks of my income. (One report says that the typical American spends one-quarter of his annual income on his automobile.)

I discovered, however, that there simply weren't any good books around to tell me what I wanted to know about the used car game. Most books or pamphlets on the subject either dealt with a single facet of the process (such as the prices of used cars or the ratings of specific models) or were written by experts in the field of auto sales or auto mechanics and were simply too complicated and/or poorly written for me to find useful. I wanted to know some basics – like about how much my monthly payments would be for different kinds of car loans, or a simple explanation of how much money I should expect to lose each year from depreciation.

Not finding such a book, I decided to write one myself. Unlike most people who write about cars, I am not a car buff with an abiding love for automobiles. About the only passion cars arouse in me is anger – anger when my car breaks down, anger when I feel ripped off at a repair garage, anger when I observe what the automobile has done to the air of our cities and the face of our countryside.

Despite those feelings about cars in general, I see them as a necessary evil and do not share the utopian dream of eliminating them in the short run. My concern is to make my own car as little a part of my life as possible. I want it to start when I turn the ignition and take me where I need to go without incident. And I am concerned that I be able to buy a reliable used car with as little hassle as possible.

My approach has been that of a journalist, using skills I have developed over the past half-dozen years as a full-time political reporter for newspapers and magazines. I have interviewed dozens of people directly involved in the used car business – salesmen, dealers, mechanics, consumer advocates and government officials. I have read everything I could find on the subject – books, pamphlets, and reports, including nearly 1,000 pages of documents related to the Federal Trade Commission's extensive study of the used car business. And I have spent countless hours scouring used car lots and checking out cars for various friends and acquaintances who asked me to help them find a good used car.

I know a lot more than when I met Bernie, but I still have much to learn. You can help by conveying your experiences and information about buying and selling used cars by writing me in care of the publisher (Chronicle Books, 870 Market Street, Suite 915, San Francisco, California 94102). Your contributions will be included in future editions of this book.

A few words about my biases: I think people should buy a used car only as a last resort. That is why the next two chapters examine all the other options – public transportation, rented cars, leased cars, new cars, or fixing up your current car. At the same time, I realize that used cars make sound economic and practical sense for most adult American consumers, including myself. About 75 percent of all cars on the road were purchased as used vehicles, and more than 13½ million used cars are bought and sold each year. In view of the inflated prices of new cars, I think that the trend towards used cars will increase.

One other strong bias I have acquired after months of research into the subject of used cars is against the professional used car middlemen. Every time a used car salesman enters into the picture, the price of the car goes up. The amount typically bitten off by the used car middlemen is reflected in the difference between a car's wholesale and retail prices (low and high Blue Book values), a subject I discuss in detail in Chapters 3 and 9. That difference means hundreds of millions of dollars each year that these people rake off from the public. I am convinced that if more consumers understood how the used car business operates, there would be little need for these middlemen.

I don't mean to imply that I think most used car salesmen are crooks or that they run their businesses any more illegitimately than do most other small businesspeople in the country. In the course of interviewing dozens of used car salesmen, managers, and wholesalers, I found them to be, on the whole, honest and likeable people. I've painted the portraits of some of the more

PRIVATE PARTY CARS
wheels & deals
RENT DISPLAY SPACE HERE
Wheels &Deals
583-4320
WHERE BUYER MEETS SELLER
ELCAMINO

Wheels & Deals.

Rick Jacobs thinks his Wheels & Deals business provides car buyers and sellers with a viable alternative to the traditional used car middleman. Someone with a car to sell can take the vehicle to the Wheels & Deals lot, pay a fee of $100 and leave it there for a month. During that time, prospective buyers can inspect the car, which is marked with all the important information about the car – its make, model, year, mileage, options, selling price, and other comments from the owner. If the buyer is interested, he or she can phone the car's owner and try to make a deal.

"We only rent space," Jacobs declares. "We are not a car dealership; we don't get involved in any negotiating. That is between the seller and people interested in the car."

In fact, Jacobs claims that when he helped to start Wheels & Deals seven years ago, "The idea was to keep myself out of the car business. I did not want to sell cars." But he says he felt that there was a need for a service for people who were interested in buying and selling used cars who did not wish to either bargain with the professional used car salesmen or resort to the newspaper want ads.

"A lot of people are afraid of buying one through newspaper ads. You might call up somebody with an ad who tells you that the car is 'blue.' But when you drive a half-hour to their house, you discover that their car is sky blue rather than navy blue, which is what you had in mind. Or you might go through all the hassle to arrange an appointment with someone only to discover that the 'minor dents' they mentioned turn out to be the result of a head-on collision."

At the same time, Jacobs insists that Wheels & Deals is much easier for the car seller than newspaper want ads. "The seller can waste a day waiting for someone to show up for an appointment, but he never appears. Or he can have people come to his house only to turn around because they don't like the color of the car. Wheels & Deals avoids those problems because the buyer already knows what a car looks like before he even calls up the seller."

When potential car buyers visit Jacob's lot, they can visually inspect the cars and even start the engines on the lot. But they must contact the owner before taking the car for a test drive. Jacobs estimates that 75 percent of the cars are sold after the first test drive and that 80 percent of the cars are sold within the first month on the lot.

At present, Wheels & Deals operates three separate lots with a total capacity of between seven and eight hundred cars. That's a far cry from its early days when Jacobs rented a movie drive-in parking lot on weekends and operated the business as a kind of auto flea market. "One of our biggest problems in those days was making sure that people got their cars off the lots before people showed up to go to the movies."

colorful of the used car middlemen I met in Chapter 10. You will probably like some of them, too. If nothing else, most used car salesmen come across as nice guys. That's the bread-and-butter of their profession. But some of them engage in some dubious practices to fool the average consumer, and I have included details about these little-known tricks-of-the-trade so you can beware of them.

While I do not mean to question the basic integrity of used car salesmen, I feel that the main reason these people are in business is the ignorance of the car-buying public. That is why I am so encouraged by the emergence of a number of consumer-oriented institutions throughout the country which are aimed at taking the profit out of buying and selling used cars.

In some cities, such as Portland, Oregon, there are flea markets for used cars. People interested in selling their used cars take their vehicles to a large, open-air parking lot where they rent space for a nominal figure. People interested in buying used cars can then come to the car market, see the car and deal directly with the seller. I would anticipate that many more such alternatives to the used car middlemen will spring up in the coming years.

Meanwhile, I think consumers should take time to learn some of the rules and tricks of the used car game. It is not really so difficult as it may seem at the outset. With a little bit of knowledge and a lot of patience, you can play the game well. I hope this book will even make it an enjoyable game to learn and play.

2 DON'T buy a used car, unless . . .

From the title of the book, you may have concluded that I believe everyone is better off getting a used car. Hardly. Used car buying is too risky to be endorsed wholeheartedly. Besides, it is time-consuming and often emotionally aggravating.

Consider yourself lucky if I'm able to persuade you in the following pages that you ought to live without a car, rent, lease, or buy a new car. I'm sure you won't begrudge the few bucks you plunked down for the book; I've saved you more than that in the cost of aspirin alone.

THE FRIEND-OF-THE-EARTH OPTION

None of us needs to hear another lecture about how cars are unmitigated ecological disasters. Everyone knows how automobiles have defaced the countryside, polluted our cities with exhaust fumes and noise, and generally made contemporary life aggravating. As valid as these points may be, the American economy is based on the automobile. For most of us, a car is something we don't think we can live without.

But have you ever seriously considered an auto-less existence? Have you thought of trading in your gas-guzzler for a bicycle? Have you thought of only using taxis and/or rented cars and/or public transportation?

We often think that in the long run it is cheaper and more convenient to buy and maintain an inexpensive used car than to keep shelling out money for taxis and rented cars. But is it?

Consider Eric's decision to live without owning a car.

Eric

Eric lives about two miles from his office in Washington, D.C., and enjoys frequent weekend trips to the country. So much so that he leaves his home an average of three weekends a month and drives to such places as a resort in Harper's Ferry, West Virginia, to the Skyline Drive area of Virginia, or to a beach in Maryland. His weekend excursions alone add up to nearly 10,000 miles a year of car travel. Eric also drove to his office every day and in the evenings to the movies or concerts or to friends' houses.

One evening three years ago, Eric sat down at home with a note pad. He had just retrieved his car from a repair shop where he had had his brake linings replaced for about $75. While the car was being fixed, he had borrowed a friend's bicycle to ride to his office. He enjoyed cycling to work so much that he decided to calculate whether he could live without his car altogether.

Eric computed that he was spending about $2,500 a year for his car. After checking the weekend rates of Budget Rent-a-Car, he figured he could rent cars three out of four weekends for a total of $1,457. He added to that figure a total of $476 he would have to spend on increased bus and taxi fare, as well as the purchase of a new $200 ten-speed bicycle. His total was still under $2,250, or nearly $250 less annually than what he was spending to care for and feed his '74 Chevy Nova.

These were Eric's calculations:

For rented cars: $25 or two days with unlimited mileage with Budget Rent-a-Car, plus $3 per trip for additional insurance, equalled $1,092 for 39 weekend trips ($975 for rental fees, $117 for insurance). Since he drove about 250 miles per excursion, he added on the price of gas for 9,750 miles. He figured the cars got about 16 mpg and gas then cost about 60¢ per gallon. This would mean another $365 a year for gas. (See Rental Option section for how to compute gas costs.) The rental total: $1,457.

For other transportation: A new ten-speed bike would cost about $200. He figured he'd have to take a bus to work about three months a year during inclement weather. This would be $60 in bus fares (50¢ each way for 60 round trips). He added another $60 for bus trips he would take for other occasions, such as to the movies in the evening. Finally, he estimated that if he took taxis three times a week, he would spend another $468 (assuming about $3 per trip at Washington's relatively cheap taxi rates). Eric's total "other transportation" costs would be $788. This plus his car rental costs would equal a grand total of $2,245.

Three weeks later, Eric sold his Nova to a new car dealer for $1,500, purchased a new Raleigh ten-speed bike and started his car-less life. At times he says he misses the convenience of being able to hop in his car and drive wherever he wants to go. On the other hand, he enjoys not having the responsibility of owning a car. He considers himself a mechanical klutz and invariably suspected he was being ripped off when he took his car to a mechanic. Eric also enjoys not having to hassle parking in downtown Washington.

Some of Eric's friends find the new auto-less Eric a bit of a social bore since he constantly tells people at parties about the glories of riding a bicycle to work. He is also in the habit of boasting about the ten pounds he's lost since selling his car.

It may be that your own situation is completely different from that of either Eric. You may not live or work near public transit, as each of them does. You may have other family members whose transportation needs necessitate owning a car. If so, you may wish to ignore the next section about renting cars. But read on if you're still not sure whether you can afford renting rather than owning a car.

THE RENTAL OPTION

A quick look at the Yellow Pages of your local phone directory will undoubtedly yield numerous companies from which you can rent a car. In the Chicago, Illinois, phone book, for instance, I counted 61 separate companies that rent cars, many of which had several branch offices (Budget listed 46 locations). Rental companies run the gamut, from big national chains like Hertz and Avis to businesses that rent used cars (such as "Rent-A-Heap-Cheap" and "Drive a Wreck"). There's even a company called "Rent-A-Rolls" for those who want to indulge their more extravagant fantasies.

As the price of new cars escalates, renting and leasing cars is becoming increasingly common. It is no longer a sport for the jet-setting O. J. Simpsons who rent while on out-of-town business trips with business expense accounts. Some car experts estimate that 10 percent of all new cars are purchased by companies for rental or leasing (more on leasing below). In the next decade, these experts claim the figure may rise to 40 percent.

ANTI-SMOG
DEVICE

Charlie Starbuck and His "Anti-Smog Device"

Ten years ago, Charlie Starbuck, an attorney and San Francisco City Planning Commissioner, got fed up with the hassles of parking and maintaining his MGB sports coupe in the city. So he sold his car for $1,500 and bought a ten-speed bike to use in its place.

He is shown here with his third bike — a ten-speed $200 Japanese Centurion model — which he rides to all of his business appointments and social engagements. (His first bike eventually wore out; his second got stolen.) Charlie only rides a bus on particularly rainy days or when he makes trips across the San Francisco Bay to Berkeley or Oakland. He sticks out his thumb and hitches rides when he wants to take a camping trip to the Sierra mountains. About twice a year, he rents a car to take friends on visits outside the city.

Charlie finds bicycling more efficient than car travel because he doesn't have to spend time parking. But mostly he's attracted to it because of the economics. Last year he only spent $15 on bicycle repairs. He calculates he paid a grand total of only $235 for all his transportation needs last year ($70 for bicycle depreciation, $15 for bike repairs, $75 on city bus fares, $15 on BART train fares, and $60 on car rentals).

Bikes have their drawbacks, however. Charlie says he doesn't appreciate water splashing from his rear wheel on to the back of his neck when the roads are wet. And it took him a while to get accustomed to parked motorists unexpectedly opening their car doors in front of him, and buses cutting him off in traffic or taxis making sudden stops in his path. Though he's had lots of near misses, Charlie has yet to take a spill. "Once you get used to riding in city traffic, a bike is no more dangerous than a car," he insists.

Charlie feels his "anti-smog device" is fighting air pollution. "Most of the people I know in the city use their cars for fairly short trips. All experts say that it's stop-and-go driving and idling cars that contribute the most pollutants."

Like virtually anything related to cars, the rental field is full of quick-talk salespeople. Most people inexperienced with renting cars have probably had the uncomfortable sensation of walking into a rent-a-car agency only to discover that the $11.95 rate they heard quoted over the phone was only a third of what they ultimately spend to rent the car. They suspect that somewhere between the mileage surcharge and the collision insurance, they've been ripped off.

What follows is a short guide to help you sort out the dollars and cents of the car rental field and help you determine whether it's a viable option for your automotive needs.

BASIC RATE

This is the amount you hear advertised and invariably have quoted to you on the phone. Although it is only the initial cost, there are several factors that affect it:

Car size: Virtually all rent-a-car companies vary their basic rate according to the car model and size. It's cheaper for you to rent a subcompact car like a

Chevette or a Pinto than a mid-sized car like a Chevrolet Malibu or a Ford Fairmont. (Some companies classify the same car differently, however. I discovered that some called a Fairmont "mid-sized" while others offered a slightly cheaper rate for the same car as a "compact.")

You can expect the basic rate to jump a couple of dollars for each step in car size. If, for instance, the basic rate for a subcompact is $15 per day, a mid-sized car from the same company might cost between $18 and $20.

Some large national companies have a full selection of car sizes. Hertz, for example, has the following range: subcompact, compact, mid-sized, full-sized, full-sized wagon, premium, and luxury.

When rented: Most car rental agencies, particularly the big national ones, also vary their basic rates according to when you pick up the vehicle. They expect businesspeople on expense accounts to rent cars during the week. So they reduce their weekend rates to encourage ordinary people to use rental cars on weekends. The rental agencies figure that the cars would otherwise remain idle on the weekends while the companies still have to pay for the depreciation costs. (It's the same principle employed by the major airlines, which offer substantial savings on midnight flights.)

The weekend rates are often 25 percent or less than the weekday rates. National for instance, charged $21.26 a day in Cleveland, Ohio, for a compact Chevrolet Nova rented on a weekday but $15 per day on weekends.

Two other points to remember about weekend rates. Companies differ on how they define "the weekend." Some offer weekend rates for cars picked up on Thursdays, while other consider Friday afternoon or even Saturday morning to be the start of the weekend. Also, some companies will give you the weekend rates only if you plan to use the car for at least two days. For instance, as shown in my survey (Table 2.1), Budget Rend-A-Car offers a daily weekend subcompact rate that is $2 cheaper ($11.95) than Avis's ($13.95). But you need to keep the car at least two days to qualify for Budget's lower rate, while Avis offers its rate for one-day outings.

Most companies also offer weekly rates that are usually considerably cheaper on a daily basis than their basic weekday rates. Some also offer special holiday rates at certain times of the year. Note, however, that some of the special rates only apply if you return the car to the same location from which you rented it. Make sure you understand the terms of the return of the vehicle. Otherwise you may have to pay a "drop charge" (see Drop Charge, below).

Where rented: The nationwide car rental companies charge different rates for different cities, and in some cases, different rates within the same area (charging slightly less at times for suburban or airport rentals than those from the city center locations). For a mid-sized Ford Fairmont rented for one weekday, Hertz charged $23 and 25¢ a mile in Kansas City, $24 and 26¢ per mile in San Francisco, and $26 and 35¢ a mile in New York City.

Mileage Surcharge versus Unlimited Mileage

You should *always* avoid renting a car when you have to pay a mileage surcharge. It is stated in terms of cents per mile. For instance, if you rent a mid-sized car from Hertz, you might be charged $24 a day plus 26¢ per mile. A subcompact car might cost $20 per day plus 20¢ per mile, while a luxury car might cost $31 a day plus 33¢ per mile.

For a hundred-mile trip, you would typically have to pay more for the mileage surcharge than for the basic rate. Using Hertz's mid-sized rental car as an example, you would have to pay $24 for the basic rate but $26 for 100 miles with a mileage surcharge of 26¢ per mile.

Some companies offer a certain number of "free miles" before charging you with a mileage surcharge. This can make a rental deal particularly attractive if you anticipate driving less than the maximum number of "free miles."

There are two common ways to beat the mileage surcharge. First, for their weekend customers the major national car rental companies generally offer rates with "unlimited mileage," the industry's term for no mileage surcharge. For a slightly higher basic rate, some also offer unlimited mileage for weekly rentals. Avis, for instance, quoted me a price of $132.60 plus 24¢ a mile to rent a mid-sized Ford Fairmont or Chevrolet Nova for a week. But for $147, I could rent the same car with unlimited mileage. Unless you anticipate driving less than 60 miles a week, it would pay to spend the extra $14.40 for the higher basic rate to obtain the unlimited mileage provision.

The second way to beat the mileage surcharge is to rent from a local or smaller regional rent-a-car agency that tries harder by offering unlimited mileage as a means of competing with the heavy advertising budgets of the Big Four (Hertz, Avis, National, and Budget). If you are seriously interested in renting cars as an alternative to owning one, you should comb the Yellow Pages of your phone directory to find out about these companies. For the price of a local phone call, you can easily learn their rates.

Drop Charge

Also called a "one-way service fee," a drop charge is often added to your bill if you return the car to a different office than the one where you rented it. Some of the big companies don't charge anything extra if you deliver the car to another major city but will make you pay extra surcharge to give it back to them at a smaller city. Avis, for example, would charge nothing for a mid-sized car rented in Chicago and left off in St. Louis. But Avis would charge an extra $25 for the same car rented in Chicago and deposited in Des Moines, Iowa.

Note also that many of these companies also charge an "unauthorized

4140

Simeon White, Noncar Owner

Simeon White recently decided to buy a used car. He had not owned an automobile since his move from Philadelphia to San Francisco five years ago. Since he didn't need a car to drive to work and he lived near a major bus stop, he never got around to buying another one.

In recent months, however, Simeon has grown increasingly fond of the scenic beaches and mountains of northern California, especially some of the nude beaches south of the city. Unfortunately, his favorite spots on the coast and in the mountains are inaccessible by public transportation. So he has either had to hitch a ride in a friend's car or rent one at what seem to him to be exorbitant rates. He has also found it more and more inconvenient to travel to places in the city at night and has often called a taxi to get home.

When Simeon asked me to help him buy a used car, I suggested we first sit down and figure out exactly how much he now spends for transportation. After adding all his costs together, we discovered that even with rented cars and taxi trips, his annual total was only $409 – less than I currently spend for car insurance alone!

Simeon's costs were as follows: $132 a year for bus fare; $17 for occasional train fare; $60 a year for taxis (averaging one $5 trip each month); $200 a year for rented cars ($25, including gas, for eight one-day rentals). Total: $409.

I told Simeon he could expect to spend at least three times his $409 just to maintain an old clunker, like the '65 Dart I used to own. I looked up the detailed expense records I had kept in 1977 and saw that I spent a total of $1,254 (including gas, repairs, insurance) although I drove the car only about 7,500 miles – three-fourths the national average. The Internal Revenue Service, for instance, uses the estimate of 17¢ per mile for the average expenses for the typical driver. At that rate, a driver would spend $1,700 for 10,000 miles a year.

With the price of gas rising, I doubt that many drivers spend less than $1,000 a year for a car, with the possible exception of the few people with fully paid-off vehicles they only drive to church on Sunday mornings. In fact, the typical 10,000-mile-a-year automobile owner whose car averages about 16 mpg would spend more than $600 in fuel costs alone, with gas priced at one dollar a gallon.

Faced with the economic facts of owning an automobile, Simeon concluded he'd rather throw his transportation money at Avis and Yellow Cab than buy a used car. He estimated he could rent a car every other weekend and still spend less than $1,000 a year for all his transportation costs.

return location fee" of at least $25 if you leave the car at a spot you did not originally specify. That's to keep you from abandoning the car and making them find it.

Insurance

Virtually all rental companies provide liability, collision and comprehensive insurance for their cars as part of the basic rate. Although the liability coverage – insurance for you in case you cause damage to someone else or another vehicle – is generally adequate, the rental companies do not generally insure you for 100 percent of the damage done to your rented car if the vehicle is involved in a collision, fire, theft, or vandalism. In such cases, you would normally have to pay the first $250 to $350 of any damage to the rented car while you have it.

If you want to make sure you don't have to pay a cent to have the rented car fixed in case of an accident or other catastrophe, the rental companies offer a policy to cover you completely. The typical charge is $3 for this total insurance coverage.

Note: If you already own a car and have comprehensive and collision insurance coverage, you may be covered under its provisions. Call your own insurance agent to find out.

You can take a gamble and not buy the extra insurance. When I've rented a car for just a day or two for a trip outside of a city, I haven't bothered with the additional insurance. But when I've rented a car for a week or planned to use it to drive around a city, I have bought the extra coverage. Just remember to add the extra $3 for the insurance to your total costs for renting if you decide to take it.

Some companies also offer a major medical benefits insurance package to cover occupants of your rented car in case of an accident. This is unnecessary if you already have complete medical insurance. But again, this is a matter of personal preference. The rate usually runs between $1.50 and $2 for this coverage.

Gas Costs

Most rental companies make you pay for your own gas. You take the car out with a full tank and are supposed to return it with a full tank. If not, you'll have to reimburse the rental agency for the difference, meaning they'll fill it up for you at their premium gas rates.

In any event, you should also calculate how much gas you will need while renting the car if you want to know how much the trip will cost. The calculation is relatively simple, especially if you have any idea what kind of gas mileage (mpg) your rented car normally gets.

Most car rental agencies can provide you with the federal Environmental Agency estimates of the mpg for specific car models they rent. (You can also obtain the same information directly from the EPA. See Chapter 12.)

Once you know the EPA's estimate of a specific car's mpg, you can make a rough calculation of your gasoline costs. The formula is simple: Divide your estimate of the miles you intend to travel by the EPA mpg estimate, then multiply that total by the price per gallon of gasoline. Or:

$$\frac{\text{miles you intend to travel}}{\text{car's mpg}} \times \text{price per gallon}$$

Suppose you want to drive your rented Ford Fairmont one hundred miles, and gas costs $1 per gallon. The EPA estimate for the Fairmont is 16 mpg. To determine your gas costs, you would divide one hundred miles by 16 mpg and multiply by $1, for a total estimated gas cost of $6.25. The same trip in a Chevette (25 mpg, according to the EPA) would cost $4.

Eligibility

Most car rental agencies won't hand you the keys of a five-thousand-dollar machine without some kind of assurance you'll return it. You'll need to have a valid driver's license and be over 21 years of age. If you don't have a major credit card, such as Visa or Master Charge, some agencies make it difficult. Hertz, for instance, says that without a major credit card, you need to present evidence that you've been employed by the same company for at least one year and put down a deposit of $50 or pay the full amount of your estimated rental costs before you take the car. Some other companies simply won't rent you a car without a major credit card or a huge deposit.

If you expect anyone other than someone in your immediate family to drive the car, he or she must be with you when you pick up the car and sign the rental agreement. Otherwise they would not be covered by the insurance and you may find yourself liable for a whopping lawsuit in case of an accident in which the other person was driving.

Shop Around!

Car rental sales agents are probably among the most pleasant people around. With a local phone call, you can quickly discover the rates of renting almost any car for any length of time. The sales agents are accustomed to quoting prices over the phone and see that as one of their primary jobs. So don't feel bashful about asking. The Big Four rental companies also have toll-free nationwide numbers (area code 800) with sales agents on duty twenty-four hours a day. Many local and regional car rental agencies also have someone ready to quote you prices in the evenings, on weekends, and even in the middle of the night.

To dramatize how much can be saved by doing a little shopping by phone, I've compiled a chart based on price quotations I received by phone from eight car rental agency offices located in San Francisco. The first four are major nationwide chains (Hertz, Avis, National, and Budget). The fifth (Dollar) is a smaller national chain. The sixth (Bay Area Rent-a-Car) is a local company with seven outlets. The last two only rent used cars (Rent-a-Wreck and Rent-a-Heap-Cheap).

To make a fair comparison, I asked for the rates each company would charge for a mid-sized Fort Fairmont as well as for a subcompact Chevette. I've assumed a one-day weekday trip of 100 miles, and added the cost of gas,

using the EPA estimates and $1 per gallon. I have not included the price of optional insurance.

If nothing else, the chart dramatizes the significance of "unlimited mileage." The weekday rates of the Big Four include mileage surcharges. This accounts for the drastic difference in costs between those companies' weekday and weekend rates – on a weekend the cost of renting a car from Hertz, Avis, National, or Budget is less than half the cost of renting on a weekday. This is why the Big Four's weekend rates are so competitive with the smaller agencies' rates.

Note: This chart is only meant to demonstrate the importance of shopping around. You should not read it to mean that Hertz invariably has the highest weekday price and your local "Rent-a-Wreck" always has the lowest. Car rental prices are constantly changing, and the companies are always adding special rates of various sorts to attract customers.

Brenn Lea Pearson and her Kawasaki 400

Though she had owned a car from the age of eighteen, Brenn Lea Pearson decided to get rid of her last car, a Ford van, in favor of a motorcycle when she was twenty-seven. At the time, she had recently moved into a big city. That was nearly seven years ago, and Brenn Lea has no intention of returning to an automobile for her transportation needs.

"A motorcycle saves time," testifies Brenn Lea. "When I go downtown, I can park my motorcycle where I am going. I don't have to waste all the time and energy looking for a parking space."

Equally important, Brenn Lea claims using a motorcycle saves her a lot of money. Last year, she estimates that she spent just over $500 for all of her expenses related to her motorcycle. Nearly half of that ($228) was for her insurance policy, which included liability, collision ($150 deductible), and theft. Since her cycle gets nearly 50 mpg, her gas expenses are not great. And maintenance on her Kawasaki 400 has consisted only of two tune-ups a year ($30 to $35 each), though this year she had to purchase a new battery for about $30. When added together, Brenn Lea figures that her motorcycle costs only about ten or eleven cents a mile – about half what most automobile owners spend for transportation.

Brenn Lea bought her 1975 model year Kawasaki 400 in 1976 as a used vehicle from a motorcycle dealer for about $750. She had bought a new cycle of the same type a year earlier for $1,000, but someone stole it. In addition to buying the motorcycle, Brenn Lea also purchased a helmet ($30), some heavy leather gloves ($25), and some rain gear ($30).

In her years of riding motorcycles (her first experience was at the age of twenty-one), Brenn Lea has been involved in only one accident. That happened six years ago when she was rear ended by a car while she was stopped to pay a bridge toll. She was not injured, and the accident cost only about one hundred dollars for repairs, which the car driver paid for.

"I suppose riding a motorcycle is a lot more dangerous than a car," Brenn Lea observes. "Drivers either do not see you, or they are purposefully out to get you. But you have a lot more awareness on a motorcycle than in a car. You can see much better; you have better peripheral vision; and you have a lot more control. It's classic defensive driving."

Brenn Lea rides her motorcycle almost every day, both around the city and occasionally on long trips into the country. "Every few days, I go on a long ride just for the feel of it, especially if I've had a rotten day.

"I cannot imagine living without a motorcycle. It would be like being immobile."

How To Compare Rental Rates

You don't need a pocket calculator to compare rent-a-car rates, though it can make the job – which is merely the process of adding together three or four figures – a little easier.

Specifically, the comparison process involves adding the basic rate, the mileage surcharge (if any), insurance or other surcharges, sales tax, and the cost of gasoline. In the example of the 100-mile weekday trip in the rented Hertz Ford Fairmont, I arrived at a total of $59.50 by the simple addition:

$24.00	Basic rate
26.00	Mileage surcharge (26¢ times 100 miles)
3.25	Sales tax (6.5 percent times $50)
6.25	Gas (100 miles divided by 16 mpg times $1 a gallon)
$59.50	Total

Car Rental Comparison Chart—One-Day Rates, 100-Mile Trip

(includes mileage surcharge, sales tax, gas estimate)

		Hertz	Avis	National	Budget	Dollar	Bay Area	Rent-A Heap	Rent-A Wreck
Ford Fairmont (16 mpg, EPA)	weekday	$59.50	$52.80	$50.93	$49.25	$31.76	$30.22	$19.84[d]	$18.99[e]
	weekend	25.37	23.24	23.24[a]	21.11[a]	31.76	26.19[c]	19.84[d]	18.99[e]
Chevette (25 mpg, EPA)	weekday	46.60	42.29	40.16	39.10	23.62[b]	21.49	19.84[d]	18.99[e]
	weekend	18.86	18.86	19.93[a]	16.73[a]	23.62[b]	21.49	19.84[d]	18.99[e]

a. Two-day minimum. b. Pinto only (22 mpg, EPA) c. Nova only (13 mpg, EPA) d. '69-'73 American cars with automatic transmission (12 mpg estimate) e. '63-'72 American cars with automatic transmission (12 mpg estimate)

Here's a blank form to help you calculate your own comparisons:

________ Basic rate (______ times number of days ______)
________ Mileage surcharge (______ times estimated trip mileage of ______ miles)
________ Insurance (Extra comprehensive ______, medical ______, other ______)
________ Extra fees (drop charge ______, other ______)
________ *Subtotal (add the above items)
________ *Sales tax (multiply subtotal of ______ times ______ percent local sales tax rate)
________ *Gas estimate (miles of trip ______, divided by EPA estimated mpg for your model of rental car ______mpg, multiplied by the average price per gallon ______)
________ Total (add subtotal, sales tax and gas)

3 TO LEASE or not to lease?

Still not convinced you should stay out of the used car market? Perhaps you haven't looked at the pros and cons of leasing or buying a new one. But first, maybe you should consider holding onto your old car and fixing it up.

FIX YOUR CURRENT CAR

Even Detroit has been unable to perfect instant obsolescence. With regular maintenance, and barring a major accident, most cars should last ten years and 100,000 miles. That's an important fact to remember if you're planning to get rid of your present automobile.

Jane and her Comet

An acquaintance of mine named Jane owned her Mercury Comet for four-and-a-half years when it suddenly broke down last winter. At the time it collapsed, she was driving across town to pick up her children from school. So she was especially upset at being stranded and having to get her car towed to a nearby garage while simultaneously having to make arrangements to have a neighbor pick up her children.

Jane got the Comet new in 1973 for about $2,500 and had had relatively few problems. But her Comet already had suffered what she considered to be two other major repairs in 1978 – a brake job for $85 and a new muffler for $50. When the garage mechanic told her that the shaft on the automatic transmission of her Comet had broken and would cost about $400 to replace, Jane concluded that this was the final straw. She'd just have to sell her Comet and get another car.

Jane faced the classic car owner's dilemma: Sell the Comet before it becomes a major repair expense and headache? Or hold onto it and hope for the best?

Jane decided to sell the Comet. The mechanic said he had a friend who might like to buy her car "as is," meaning he'd be willing to buy it before the mechanic fixed it. The mechanic said he also had another customer who was trying to sell a '74 Chevrolet Vega station wagon "cheap." The mechanic swore the Vega was in good running shape.

Using the mechanic as a go-between, Jane sold her '73 Comet for $800 and bought the '75 Vega for $1,500. Jane thought she was getting a good deal because the Vega cost her only $300 more than she would have had to spend on the transmission job anyway. Besides, she figured, she was getting a car that was one year younger than her Comet for only $300.

Jane's story does not have a happy ending. A month after she bought the Vega, its engine overheated and had to be replaced – for nearly $1,000. She went to the garage to complain to the mechanic for selling her a lemon. But the garage mechanic had quit a few weeks earlier and nobody seemed to know how to locate him.

In the ensuing six months, Jane sent her Vega to the shop three times for repairs totaling another $225. Mention "Vega" in her presence and she gets red in the face. (I called the new owner of her Comet. He reported that the car runs well and has had no further problems.)

In retrospect it's obvious Jane should have held onto her Comet. But are there any general principles to help you decide whether to keep or sell your current car?

Here is my three-step method to help you resolve your to-sell-or-not-to-sell dilemma:

Step 1 *Have a competent mechanic give your current car a complete check-up.* He should do a compression test to see if you will need a major engine repair soon. He should look at other major potential repair problems: the transmission, clutch, rear-end brakes and suspension. Most major auto problems give distinctive warning signs in advance of a breakdown. Once you've had it checked out, you should have a good idea how much your car would cost you in major repairs.

Step 2 *Find out how much your current car is worth.* Look at the newspaper want-ads to see how much your model is selling for on the private market. You can also discover how much your car would be worth by calling a few new or used car dealers. They will tell you its low "Blue Book" price, or its wholesale worth. (See Chapter 9 for more on this subject.)

Step 3 *Determine how much a replacement car might cost.* Check the newspaper ads for costs of specific models. Or you can call new or used car dealers to find out how much certain models would cost. Assume you can, to some extent, bargain down the private parties or the dealers. (See Chapter 9, "The Art of Haggling.")

Once you've gone through these three steps, you'll be in a better position to make a rational decision about your current car. Of course, there are a multitude of intangibles that always enter into such a decision – your desire to drive something that *looks* newer, your dissatisfaction with your current car's options or styling, your attachment to your car's quirks, to mention a few.

Keep in mind that if you decide to keep your car, you can improve it. If you've discovered that you're probably better off holding onto your current car for another two years, you're probably going to save several hundred dollars in the short run. So you might do as my friend Lillie did recently.

Lillie had a cream-colored '69 Volkswagen Beetle that needed a new engine. After determining that it made more sense to her financially to put in a new engine (for $500) than to get another car, Lillie decided to spend another $150 and have her Bug repainted bright red. (A cheap repainting costs less than $100.) Now Lillie drives her same VW bug, but it *feels* like a new car because it's a different color.

LEASING

Leasing a brand new car may suit you better than buying a used one. Especially if it would cost you less money in both the short- and long-run.

Most individual consumers have unfortunately considered leasing to be the private reserve of financial wizards and big corporations. To be sure, many companies have made a practice of leasing cars because they figure that by leasing, they tie up less capital in vehicles than they would if they purchased them. But there's no reason that the same principle won't work for you.

Leasing is a combination of renting and purchasing a car. When you lease a car, you agree to pay a specific monthly rate for a certain time period. In that respect, leasing is like renting an apartment or a house. For instance, I called a local Ford dealer who told me I could lease a brand-new four-door Ford Fairmont with manual transmission (retail price $5,300) for a monthly rate of $125 a month for 36 months.

Unlike most housing rental arrangements, however, I would have total responsibility for the vehicle during the time I leased it. In this respect, leasing is different from renting a car from Hertz or some other car rental agency since those companies assume all of the maintenance costs of the vehicle. In other words, when leasing a car, you normally have to pay for all maintenance costs (oil changes, lubes, and so forth), repairs and insurance during the leasing period, just as if you had purchased the car. Note, however, that the car would be covered by the same factory new car warranty as any other brand-new car.

The most complicated aspect of leasing relates to your agreement with the leasing company about what happens to the car at the end of the leasing period. The simplest option is a *closed-end lease* where you simply return the car to the leasing company with no strings attached. This is also known as a walk-away lease or a fixed-cost lease.

A closed-end lease is generally less desirable than an *open-end lease*, which gives you the options of returning the car, buying it, or selling it yourself. In most open-end leases, the crucial factor is the leasing company's original estimate of the car's value at the end of the leasing period.

Let's look at the example of the Fairmont lease I mentioned above. The salesman told me that at the end of the 36-month lease, his dealership estimated that the car would be worth $2,800. So he would write into my leasing agreement that at the end of 36 months I could:

1 Buy the car for $2,800; or

2 Sell the car privately and pay his dealership $2,800; or

3 Return the car to the dealership. If the dealership appraised the car for $2,800 at that time, we would be even and I would have no further dealings with the company. But if the company appraised the car for less than $2,800, I would have to pay the difference.

Note: There are laws limiting your liability in case the leasing company appraises the car at less than their original estimate when you return it. Usually the law limits your liability to three times the average monthly payment. In the Fairmont lease agreement this means that, since the monthly payment is $125, no more than $375 could be added to the $2,800 estimate. This does not take into account what happens in case the car is severely damaged.

Many people take advantage of the second option because they think they can sell the car for more than the company's original estimate. This can work to your advantage particularly well if you happen to lease a very expensive car that depreciates slowly. See the photo of Tom Parker, who hopes to sell his '79 BMW for $10,000 at the end of his leasing period but only has to pay his leasing company $6,000.

Advantages of Leasing

There are several advantages of leasing over buying a new or used car:

1 You have less money tied up in the car since you may have no down payment or only a comparatively small one.

2 Your monthly payments are often considerably less than loans for a comparably sized new car. Often this means that for the same amount of money, you can be driving a fancier vehicle.

The reason the monthly payments are lower is simple. You are paying a loan on the estimated depreciation of the car during the leasing period rather than on the full value of the car. In other words, you pay a loan on the difference between the retail price ($5,300 in the case of the Fairmont) and the leasing company's estimate of its future value ($2,800 in the same example).

3 Unlike those who purchase a used car, you have the advantage of buying a new car with a factory warranty. (Some companies also lease used cars.)

4 If you use your car for business purposes, the IRS has made it extremely attractive since you can deduct the whole amount of your leasing payments from your taxable income.

Disadvantages of Leasing

Before you run out to the nearest car leasing agency, however, note that leasing has some definite disadvantages as well:

1 You need extremely good credit to lease a car. Few leasing companies will hand over a brand-new vehicle for a couple of hundred bucks. (Many companies only require the first and last month's payments in advance.) They insist on knowing that you will be able to pay the monthly installments and often have higher standards than banks or finance companies giving loans for new or used cars.

B M W

Tom Parker and his Leased BMW

How would you like to drive a brand new $12,000 car without putting any money down and only pay $47 a month? That's exactly what Tom Parker claims he can do by leasing instead of buying his car.

Here's how. Tom marched into a local BMW dealer and told a salesman he'd like to lease a car. The dealer suggested that Tom take a look at the cars he had in stock and decide which one he liked best. After test driving a few cars, Tom picked a beige two-door BMW 320i, which retails for nearly $12,000.

The salesman told Tom that his dealership did not lease directly but through a local bank. Tom filled out the application with the dealer. Since Tom had an excellent credit history, the bank approved his application within a few days.

When Tom returned to the dealership to complete the necessary forms and pick up the car, he signed the final lease that said he would be required to pay $205 a month for 48 months. In addition, the lease specified that he would have to pay his first and last months' payments when he picked up the car ($410) as well as the registration and license fees (another $150) for a total initial payment of $560.

How did Tom reduce his $205 monthly payment to only $47? Tom calculated that, although he would have to pay $205 a month up front, he would ultimately be able to deduct 1. the tax savings resulting from use of the car in his business and 2. his profit to be realized from the resale of the car.

First, his business tax deduction. As a media consultant with an office in his own home and a second automobile for personal use, Tom uses the BMW exclusively for business. This means his car expenses are legitimate business deductions for tax purposes. Congress has written the tax laws so that people or companies who lease their vehicles can deduct their entire monthly lease payments from their taxable income. This provision was written to benefit corporations which make a major practice of leasing, but it works just the same for private individuals. (In general, the IRS provisions are written to make it more advantageous for those who lease vehicles than those who use their own cars because you can deduct the entire leasing cost, whereas you can only deduct your actual car expenses of a vehicle you own.) Without going into the details of Tom's personal tax returns, Tom figures that he will eventually recoup $75 of his $205 monthly payment through this IRS provision.

How about the other $83? Tom plans to sell his BMW at the end of the leasing period and give the bank its original estimate of the car's worth. According to the terms of his lease, Tom has the option of returning the car to the dealership (bank), buying the car himself for $6,000, or selling it privately and giving the bank $6,000. (For more on options of open-end leases, see text.) Tom insists that the bank made an extremely conservative estimate when it calculated that the car would be worth only $6,000 after four years. Based on what the resale values for comparable BMWs are, and accounting for continued inflation and the relative value of the German mark versus the U.S. dollar, Tom assumes that he will easily be able to sell his BMW for $10,000 after four years. By subtracting the $6,000 he must hand over to the bank from the expected $10,000 resale value, Tom would then have $4,000. When he divides $4,000 by 48 months of his monthly lease payments, Tom estimates that he would be saving another $83 per month in his $205 monthly lease payments, for a net monthly cost of $47!

Here's a quick analysis of Tom's cheap leasing rate:

$205	monthly payment
– 75	business tax deduction
– 83	resale windfall profit
$ 47	actual average monthly lease payment

2 Like renting an apartment, you don't have anything to show for your installment payments. The car isn't yours. You don't build up equity in it, unlike buying the car.

3 You pay dearly for leasing. Take the Fairmont example of a car that sells new for $5,300 and which the company estimates will be worth $2,800 in three years. Theoretically, your monthly payments should pay for the estimated depreciation – the $2,500 difference between retail cost and the car's eventual estimated worth. Instead, you would have spent $4,500 in three years with installments of $125 a month. At that rate, you could have borrowed $3,600 at an annual interest rate of 15 percent. (See finance charts, Chapter 6.)

Where to Lease

Three types of companies offer leasing arrangements: banks, dealer-affiliated leasing companies, and independent leasing agencies. The banks typically work with individual dealers, and dealers often can offer leasing arrangements with more than one bank. Many of the big rental companies have their own leasing subsidiaries, such as Avis's We Try Harder, Inc. The Yellow Pages of your local phone book will tell you which companies operate in your community.

Because there are so many types of leases for so many types of cars, it is difficult to state any generalizations about which of the three leasing arrangements would work best to your advantage. Like renting or buying a car, it pays to be patient and shop around.

Translating Car Leasing Deals

As leasing grows in popularity, you will see more and more newspaper ads claiming that you can lease brand-new cars for what sound like incredibly low monthly payments. Unfortunately, you have to read through a lot of small print and sit down with a pocket calculator to make sense of such offers.

To give you some practice, I have taken two ads from the same morning newspaper about leases on nearly identical '79 Datsun 210s (a subcompact sedan similar to a Ford Pinto, Dodge Colt or Toyota Corolla). The ad from Dealer A states that you can lease a new Datsun 210 for "only $69 per month," while Dealer B's ad claims you can get the same car for "only $79 per month."

As can be shown in the following translation of the two ads into simple dollars and cents, the $79 per month deal is better both in the short-run and in the long-run because it doesn't require a hefty down payment (called a "Cap. reduction").

Dealer A Ad:

"DATSUN GAS CHAMP. NEW '79 210 SEDAN. ONLY $69 per month + tax.

"36 mo. Lease. Residual $2295. Advance paymt. $229, includes 1st paymt., Security dep. & lic. fee. Initial value $4,138. Total periodic paymts, $2484. Cap. reduction $560. On approval of credit."

Translation:

$2,484	Total monthly payments
161	Sales tax (6.5 percent)
560	Nonrefundable down payment ("Cap. reduction")
82	License fee ($229 "advance paymt." less $69 first monthly payment, $69 refundable security deposit, $9 sales tax on $138)
$3,287	Total cost of 36-month lease

Dealer B Ad:

"'79 DATSUN 210's. Only $79 per month.

"A total of only $179 del. incl. 1st mo. pymt., tax & license. Then 35 remaining pymts. of $79 + tax with CREDIT OK. Cap. cost $3,995; totl. per. pymts. $2,844; bring back $2,443. Brand new '79 std. 210, 4 spds, 36-MOS.: BUDGET LEASE PLAN."

Translation:

$2,844	Total monthly payments
185	Sales tax (6.5 percent)
95	License fee ($179 less first monthly payment of $79 and $5 sales tax)
$3,124	Total cost of 36-month lease

BUYING A NEW CAR

Most people who buy used cars would probably prefer to purchase a new car if they had the money. Of course, there are some who think that new cars are a rip-off since the typical standard-sized new car loses about half its value in its first three years of life. But many others see used cars as their only viable financial option.

You may feel that though you want a new car, you can't afford one. However, you might take a few minutes to check out the possibility of buying a new car. Assuming you can't shell out the full payment for a new or used car, you will undoubtedly have to pay off a loan on the vehicle. Look at the finance tables in Chapter 6 to see whether you could afford a new car loan instead. The key thing to remember is that it's generally easy to get a new car loan for a time period of 48 months, while it's often difficult to convince a bank or other financial institution to grant you more than 24 months to pay off a used car loan.

Here's one example: If you can pay about $120 a month, you might be able to borrow $2,500 for 24 months at 15 percent APR on a used-car loan ($119 to be exact). But for $111 a month at 15 percent APR, you could borrow $4,000 (enough to pay for some new subcompacts) on a 48-month loan. You would pay a lot more interest on the longer loan ($1,344 versus $410). But then again, nobody said you could get something for nothing in the car trade.

If you conclude you can buy a new car after looking at your finances, let me offer two bits of advice:

First, *shop around*. My friend Peggy recently asked me to help her get a new Volkswagen Rabbit. (She unexpectedly inherited some money and decided to put it into a new car.) She was ready to spend $6,700 for a Rabbit with her desired options at a nearby VW dealer. She incorrectly assumed that the "sticker price" on the car was sacred. She didn't understand that the dealer was charged only 80 or 90 percent of the "sticker price" (also called "suggested retail value"). So she thought that a similarly equipped Rabbit would cost the same from any dealer.

I suggested that she telephone other local VW dealers to compare prices. In a period of 20 minutes, she discovered two dealers who offered the same car for less than $6,000 and two others who charged less than $6,500.

When we went to talk to the two dealers who offered the best price over the phone, we found one who underbid the other by a hundred dollars. Peggy ultimately bought her Rabbit from that dealer for $5,800 (including taxes and license fees). That's nearly a thousand dollars in savings for a few minutes extra work!

Second, read Chapter 6 on "Putting the Bread Together" and Chapter 9 on "The Art of Haggling." You might find some useful tidbits of information that you can apply to buying a new car.

4 Are you a CLUNKER monger?

At least you're in good company if you've decided to buy a used car. Three out of every four cars you see on the road were purchased as used vehicles. Americans buy 13.5 million used cars a year, spending in excess of $21.3 billion annually.

With millions of people in the used car market every year, it's no wonder so many folks can relate stories about how they've been gypped or wound up with less than they wanted for their money. Usually they blame the person they bought the car from — hence all the "would you buy a used car from" stories. But often the real problems rest with the buyer who rushed off to the nearest used car lot and purchased the first car he or she saw.

The following two chapters are aimed at helping you to think through your own needs in a used car. While Chapter 5 relates to picking out a specific model, style and options for your car, the next few pages are meant to give you a handle on developing your own used car strategy — your own approach to the used car marketplace.

Since the most important single consideration in buying a used car is its age, the three approaches I've outlined relate to a car's age. I call the three tactical perspectives those of the *second-hander* (someone who buys used cars one to four years old), the *third-hander* (a person who buys used cars four to seven years old), and the *clunker monger* (an individual who prefers cars older than seven years).

I've outlined these three strategies to help you think through the best way to get the most for your used car dollar. Before describing some people I know who've adopted these approaches, I should explain some things about the economics of used cars, especially the all-important concept of depreciation. It's only by understanding the used car market better than others that you can beat it.

AGE AND PRICE

Nothing affects the price of used cars more than age. You've probably heard the old adage that a new car loses several hundred or even several thousand dollars once its owner drives it a block away from the showroom. If you've been around those in the used car trade, you may have heard another similar adage, that a car loses about half its value in its first three years of life.

These two expressions point out almost self-evident points about car depreciation. But the principles behind these notions are worth stating more formally – to help keep them in mind when we discuss the used car strategies.

First common-sense principle about car depreciation: Cars lose their value most rapidly during infancy, especially during their first three years of life.

Related to this concept is an important corollary:

Second common-sense principle about car depreciation: Most used car prices tend to level off after about six or seven years of life. After the age of seven, differences in price among various car models are usually related more to the condition of a car than its age or even its original price.

Once a car hits the magic age of seven, several things happen to it. First, its price is no longer listed in the "Blue Book," the all-important bible of used car salesmen. That means there is no longer any standard which new or used car dealers can use to determine the wholesale value of the car. Consequently, it becomes extremely difficult to trade in a car older than seven years to a new car dealer. (More on the Blue Book in Chapter 9, "The Art of Haggling.")

Not only does the Blue Book ignore cars older than seven, so do various consumer publications, such as Consumer Reports. That makes it difficult for the well-informed used car buyer to base his or her decision on any factual data of how well a given model performs after the age of seven.

Finally, many car manufacturers simply do not carry parts for their vehicles older than seven years since federal laws only require them to keep a stock of parts for seven years. This means that for some models, it can be extremely difficult to obtain parts, thereby decreasing their worth in the eyes of many potential buyers. This is certainly not true for all models, especially ones that change little in design from year to year, such as the older Volkswagen Beetles. (Nor does it mean you should stay away from older cars because you can't get parts for them.)

Third common-sense principle about car depreciation: It's impossible to predict in advance exactly how much a specific car model will lose its value in the course of a year.

This third point is what makes buying used cars, particularly newer model ones, especially aggravating to many newcomers to the field. But it is possible to make an educated guess about how quickly a car will depreciate. To get an idea as to how much cars depreciate annually, I picked out ten 1972 model year cars and followed their price careers over a seven-year span, using the prices listed in the *Kelley Blue Book* each year. (See Tables 4.1 and 4.2.)

I intentionally chose a broad cross-section of cars, ranging in original list price from about $2,000 to more than $7,000, and included seven American-made and three foreign cars. They also ranged in style and size, from the luxury (Mercedes-Benz 250, Cadillac DeVille) to the sporty (Ford Thunderbird and Mustang) to the standard-sized (Mercury Marquis, Buick LaSabre) to the compact (Volvo, Dodge Dart) to the subcompact (VW Beetle and Chevrolet Vega).

These tables chart both the annual changes in the cars' retail prices (high Blue Book) and in their wholesale or trade-in prices (low Blue Book). Both figures are highly relevant to any prospective used car buyer. The Blue Book's retail value is the average price that people are paying to buy a specific model; the wholesale value is the average amount people are selling their cars for.

The difference between retail and wholesale values of used cars is a crucial notion — one which is essential to master before trying to get the best bargain for a car (see Chapter 9, "The Art of Haggling"). For now, however, we should observe that in addition to the fact that most cars lose their value over time, most car owners also lose a sizeable chunk of money when they sell their cars. The difference between a car's wholesale and retail values normally equals the money bitten off by a middleman — the used car dealer. Enough on that point for the moment.

Even a cursory look at the charts illustrates that individual models vary greatly, especially with regard to the general maxim that cars lose 20 to 25 percent of their value in the first year and about 50 percent of their value in the first three years. That statement may hold true for the Cadillac DeVille, but you can see that the Mercedes-Benz 250 lost very little value after its initial drop in the first year. At the same time, you can see that the value drops in the subcompacts and compacts much less drastically than with the larger cars.

One final observation. These charts show general trends for the specific models mentioned above. You can do your own quick calculation on models you are interested in by either using back issues of the Blue Book (available in most libraries) or simply by looking at newspaper ads. In other words, if you are interested in a '77 Chevy Nova, two-door coupe, look up what the going prices in the newspaper ads are for the '76, '75, and '74 models of the same car. Although this is not as precise a method as I used, it will give you some idea of how that car is depreciating in your local market.

DEPRECIATION AND MAINTENANCE

If car owners only had to pay for depreciation, no one would be willing to fork over $4,000 and up for a new car. The financial loss suffered by removing a car from the proverbial showroom would dissuade most sane people from ever buying a new car. But most new car owners feel they are getting something besides shiny chrome and scratchless fenders in exchange for the rapid loss in car value during the first few years. Many believe they are also getting dependability and reliability. The trade-off most people perceive is depreciation versus maintenance.

Fourth common-sense principle of car depreciation: The newer the car, the more you can expect to pay for depreciation and the less for maintenance. Conversely, the older the car, the less you can expect to pay for depreciation and the more for maintenance.

Though it's not possible to make an exact prediction of car depreciation costs, you can at least make a rough estimate, as the charts in this chapter indicate. In general, you know that cars tend to level off after the age of seven or so. years and that their values tend to level off after the age of seven or so.

Not so with maintenance. Repair costs are inherently unpredictable. You might be able to drive your car for two years with no mechanical problems whatsoever, then for a stretch of six months see your water pump stop working, your alternator die, your transmission lose second gear and your muffler develop a big hole – and in addition all four tires go bald.

Despite the unpredictability of repair costs for any specified car, it is possible to make some generalizations beyond the obvious fact that repair costs tend to increase with age. The Department of Transportation did an extensive study of auto costs in a pamphlet called "Cost of Owning and Operating an Automobile," published in 1976. In the booklet, the DOT studied the average annual costs (including depreciation, maintenance, gas, parking, insurance and taxes) of cars over a ten-year span. Using the figures of the DOT study, I charted the costs for depreciation versus those of maintenance (repairs, accessories, parts, and tires). (See Tables 4.3, 4.4 and 4.5.)

Are You a Clunker Monger?

You can see from these charts that standard-sized cars tend to depreciate much more rapidly in their first few years than either compact or subcompact cars. At the same time, all three sizes of vehicles tend to have steadily increasing maintenance costs for their first four years. At that point, maintenance costs for standard and compact cars tend to increase until the seventh year while subcompact maintenance costs usually remain relatively constant through the eighth year.

Significantly, maintenance costs for all three sizes of vehicles tend to decrease after the seventh year for the standard and compact, and after the eighth year for the subcompacts. This is partly attributable to the fact that in the DOT study the researchers calculated that in its typical ten-year, 100,000-mile life, an automobile is driven fewer miles each year. According to the DOT estimate, the average car is driven 14,500 miles its first year, about 10,000 miles from its fourth through its seventh years, and only 5,700 miles in its tenth year.

Another factor may help to explain the surprisingly lower repair costs during the later years of a car's life. Put simply, it's the old Darwinian theory of *survival of the fittest*. Most cars don't live for ten years, according to a study by G. Marshall Naul that was originally printed in the magazine *Special-Interest Autos* and later excerpted in John R. Olson's book, *Make Money Owning Your Car* (Motorbooks International, Minneapolis, 1976). Naul's study of car registration for most American cars originally registered between 1946 and 1968 showed that while most models had a 90 percent survival rate after three years, only 10 percent survived 12 years and less than 1 percent lived for 16 years. For virtually all models, the sharpest drop took place after the sixth year (when even the worst models have a survival rate greater than 60 percent, and most models more than 80 percent).

I haven't discovered any hard statistical data to substantiate my conclusion based on Naul's study. But it's logical that the cars that don't get junked during those crucial seventh through tenth years are precisely the ones that can be maintained without causing outrageous repair bills as they get older.

If my survival-of-the-fittest theory sounds far-fetched, perhaps another explanation for the decreased maintenance costs will make more sense. After most cars get past the age of six or seven, they look much the worse for wear. The paint has usually faded badly; areas of the car have begun to rust; the interior upholstery begins to rip. At that point, many owners simply stop fixing all the little things that go wrong that they would fix with younger cars.

What follows is a closer look at the second-hander's, third-hander's and clunker-monger's approaches to used cars. You may be familiar with phrases applied to new car owners of an "annual trader," a "two-year trader" and a "three-year trader" – referring to how frequently the owner buys a new car. Like those approaches to cars, each of the three used car strategies has its advantages and disadvantages.

SECOND-HANDER

A friend of mine named Bonnie Butler, a school teacher in Chicago, only buys cars that are less than two years old. Recently she bought a bright red '77 Capri Ghia sports coupe for $3,200 from a man who advertised the car in a local newspaper. She told me the guy who sold her the car had to leave town soon. Although the fellow initially wanted $3,600 for the car, Bonnie got him to lower the price $400 without much difficulty.

Since the Capri sold for slightly more than $5,000 when new, Bonnie thinks she got an excellent deal. It had relatively low mileage (23,000 miles), and Bonnie's mechanic could find nothing significantly wrong with the car, though it had a dent in the right rear fender.

"Why should I buy a new car when a recent second-hand one looks and acts the same?" Bonnie asked. "I'll drive it hard for about two years and get another one. I'll save a couple thousand dollars, too."

Bonnie had been buying and selling only second-hand cars for the last ten years. She said she got stung once about six years ago when she bought a car whose automatic transmission collapsed about a month after she purchased it. Since that experience, Bonnie has been careful to have a qualified mechanic check out her purchases in advance. (More on this subject in Chapter 8, "Spotting Lemons.")

Bonnie used to buy her second-hand cars exclusively from new car dealers. She felt more confident about their cars since she could assume their stock of used cars was being replenished by "annual traders" or "two-year traders." In addition, these new car dealers invariably agreed to take her second-hand car on a trade-in basis. Despite the convenience, Bonnie has concluded that she saves more money by spending extra time and effort to buy her cars from private owners.

Bonnie is typical of many second-handers I've met. She wants a car that looks new. At the same time, she needs a reliable car since she must commute from the suburbs into the city — a total of 40 miles round-trip each day. She figures she'll get rid of the car before its maintenance costs begin to devastate her pocketbook. So she's willing to pay extra for depreciation for the two years she owns the car in exchange for anticipated lower maintenance costs.

One other facet of Bonnie's second-hand strategy: She's not very mechanically minded. She's dutiful about getting her car's oil changed, engine tuned and chassis lubricated, but she feels helpless if something goes wrong with the car. So she has traded in or sold her previous cars at the first sign of major trouble. She got rid of her '75 Toyota Celica immediately after she got its clutch fixed.

When she talks about her car-buying habits, Bonnie invariably adds one other reason for her preference for second-hand cars: *They're already broken in*. Bonnie bought her first car brand new, a '65 Ford Mustang, soon after she got her first full-time teaching job fifteen years ago. Three years later she traded it in on another new Mustang. She discovered with both cars that it took almost a year to get the kinks out of them. Though most of the minor repairs to the cars were covered by the new car warranties, she still had to take them back to the dealer numerous times for repair. (Bonnie's experience is backed up by various new car studies. One consumer publication reports that the average new car from Detroit has from six to twenty-four defects when first bought.)

From her experience with the Mustangs, Bonnie concluded that it made more sense to buy a car after it's already been driven at least 10,000 to 20,000 miles. Not only was it cheaper, but it probably would be less of a hassle to take care of.

THIRD-HANDER

My barber Roberto Perez buys what he calls third-hand cars – ones that are usually four or five years old and that typically have had two previous owners. He has a small family, so he usually purchases a four-door sedan or station wagon, like the '74 Ford Torino wagon he picked up last year for $1,500.

Roberto says his wife uses the car more than he does since he normally commutes to work by bus. Because she uses the car a great deal for errands, Roberto is concerned that the car be mechanically reliable. For that reason, he is reluctant to buy older cars or clunkers. He has also had good luck with cars like the Torino on weekend trips to the mountains or seashore.

Unlike the nonmechanically inclined Bonnie Butler, Roberto has some interest in how his car works and has done some minor repairs like cleaning and gapping the spark plugs. But he mostly relies on the mechanics in an independent repair garage located near his house on the outskirts of the city. He is confident they can take care of any problem with the car, and he has never felt ripped off in the five years he has taken his cars to them.

Roberto usually buys his cars from used car dealers. In fact, he had purchased the last three vehicles from the same dealer. As with car repairs, Roberto thinks he gets the best deal by patronizing the same car lot each time. He feels the dealer would be less likely to take advantage of him if the dealer thinks he will return for his next car. Likewise, Roberto has sold his cars to the same used car dealer, using his old car as a trade-in.

Roberto realizes he could probably save money by buying and selling his cars privately. But Roberto says, "I would rather lose a few bucks to the used car dealer than go through the hassle of doing it all myself. Besides, I always have my cousin, who used to be an auto mechanic, check out a car before I buy it.

I've never been burnt. So what difference does a couple hundred bucks mean over the three years or so I own the car? As long as it runs well, I come out ahead of the game anyway."

CLUNKER MONGER

Bill Crowe loves clunkers – cars that are older than six or seven years. "I myself would not buy a new car, even if I had the money," he says. "By buying a good used car, you can save more money. Besides that, new cars always screw up. They're always in the shop for something or other.

"What's more," he continues, "you can buy an old clunker for $300 that will run for two, three or even five years. Like my '64 Valiant. About the only repair I had to make in it this year was to replace a $30 alternator. The point is whether you want comfort or transportation."

There's even a slight ideological rationale behind Bill's preference for older cars. "I'm not into plastic," he explains. "Most new cars are made out of lots of plastic parts, while the older ones used better materials. It's even a matter of aesthetics."

Crowe is especially fond of the mid-sixties models of Dodge Darts, Plymouth Valiants, and Chevy Novas. He points to their proven durability and the easy availability of parts for these cars. His Valiant gets between 18 and 21 mpg, which he says is as good as many newer models.

Crowe is considerably more mechanically inclined than most other clunker mongers. Although he is not a professional mechanic, he has taught himself how to do even the most difficult jobs, such as a complete engine overhaul. He does not think someone needs to be as experienced as himself to own and operate an old clunker. But he thinks it helps to have more than a minimal knowledge of how a car works to avoid spending extra money in repairs.

At the same time, Bill thinks it is wise for someone buying an older car to have it checked out by a mechanic or someone who knows a lot about auto mechanics. In particular, he would not advise someone to buy a car at a public auction without the assistance of a mechanic.

With his background, Bill is able to buy cars at auctions, even when it is not possible to start the engine before purchasing a car. His checklist in such situations includes the following: He looks at the radiator to see that there is neither oil nor foam in the water, at the oil dipstick to make sure there is no water, and at the oil breather cap for any foam. Then he looks at the transmission fluid to find out whether it is red and clear. Although he cannot start the car, he tries to crank the engine by hand (using the fan pulley). If it won't move, he assumes the engine block may be cracked or frozen. Finally, he pumps down hard on the brakes to see if they work.

Bill Crowe and his "Clunker," a '64 Plymouth Valiant Convertible.

It is much easier, of course, to buy a clunker from a private party. Bill suggests that anyone interested in buying a car from someone through a newspaper ad should ask the following questions:

- How many owners has the car had?
- How long has the seller owned the car?
- Why is it being sold now?
- How many miles does it have on it?
- What price is being asked?
- Does it burn oil?
- Are the brakes good?
- Are there any other problems?

Crowe makes three final points about owning clunkers:

1 "If it runs O.K. when you get it, you can probably keep it going till you want to unload it. The trick is to make sure it runs well when you first buy it."

Janet Stock and her Patched-up Suburu "Clunker"

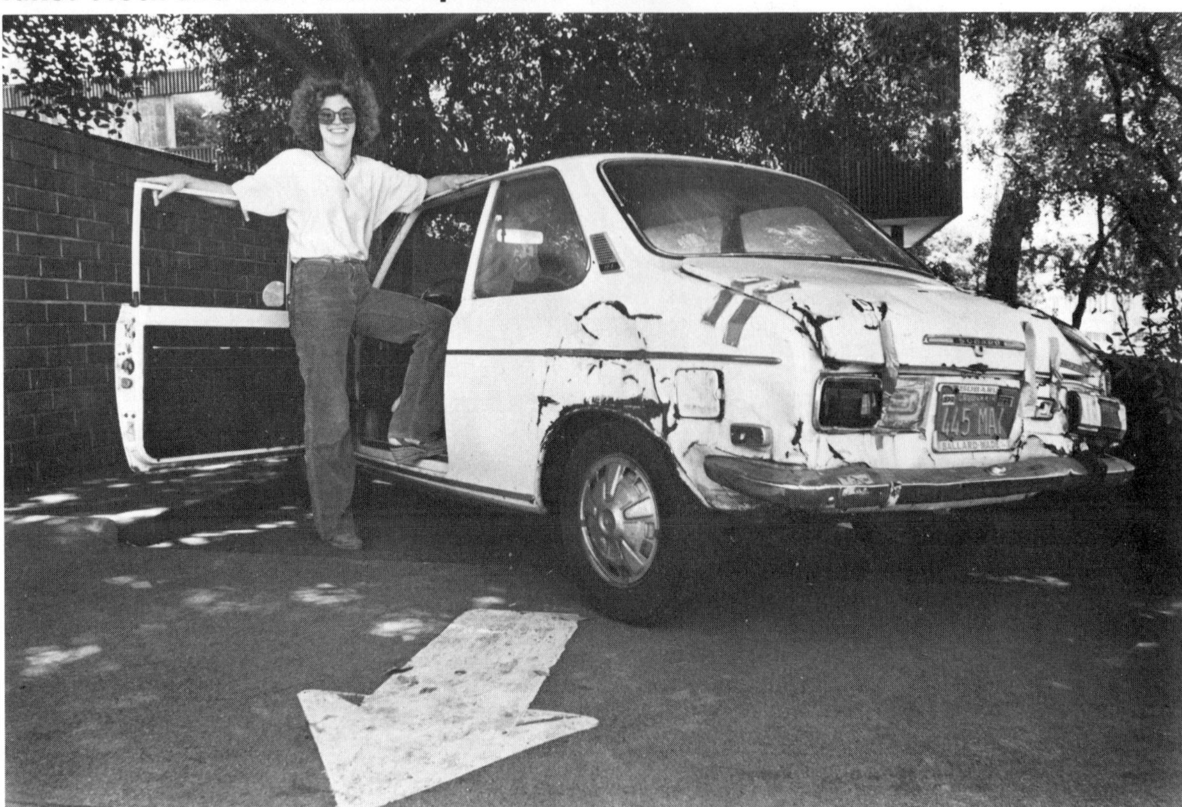

2 "Clunkers don't depreciate with age as do newer cars. You should be able to sell it for about the same as when you first bought it if you take care of it properly."

3 "Expect to get your hands greasy from time to time. It's the nature of a clunker that little things need to be fixed every now and then."

Table 4.1 Auto Depreciation (Wholesale*)

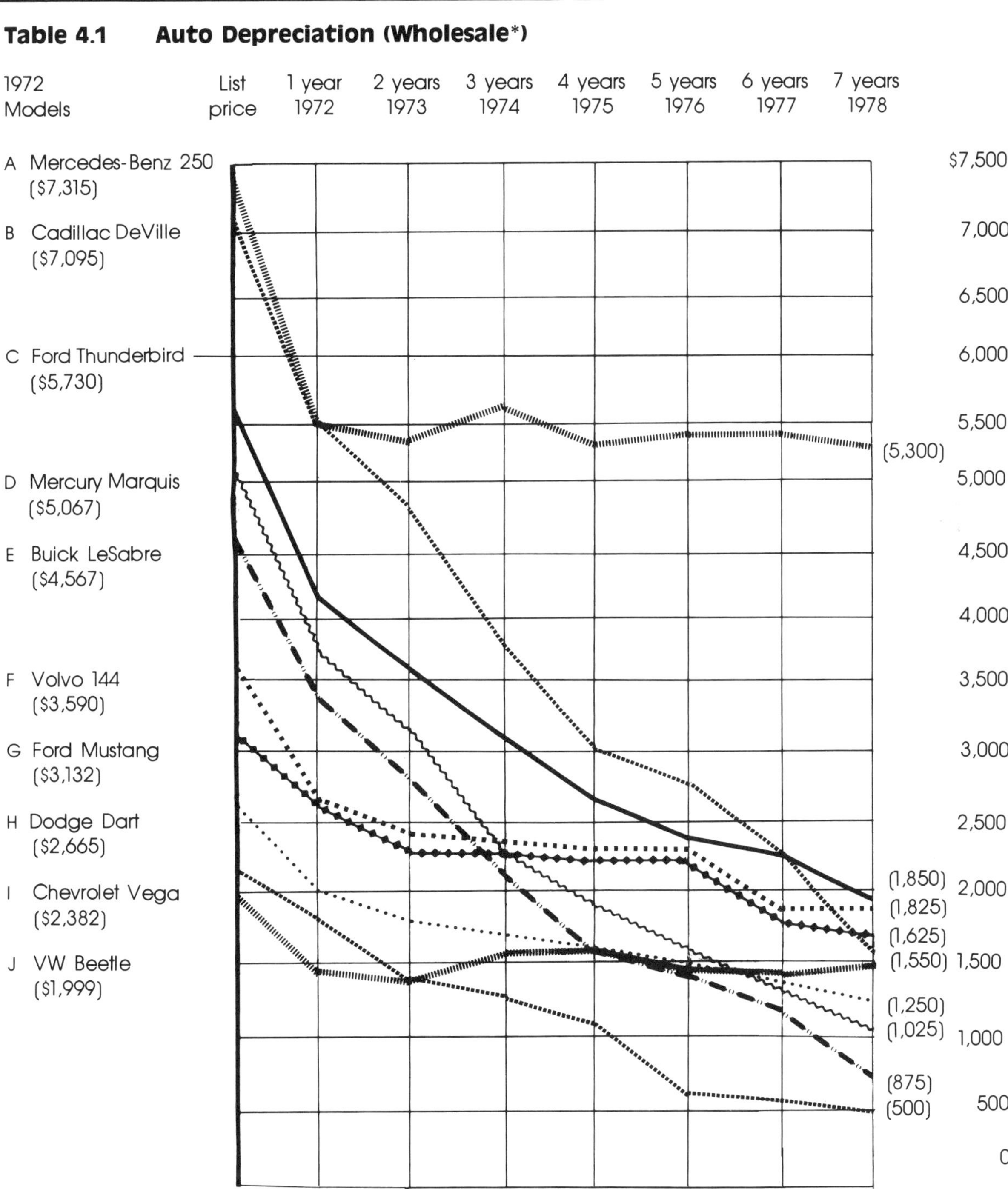

*Figures based on Kelley Blue Book wholesale values (also known as the trade-in or low book prices) as contained in the publication's September-October issues from 1972 to 1978. The list price is the model's original retail price in the fall of 1971.

Table 4.2 Auto Depreciation (Retail*)

1972 Models | List price | 1 year 1972 | 2 years 1973 | 3 years 1974 | 4 years 1975 | 5 years 1976 | 6 years 1977 | 7 years 1978

A Mercedes-Benz 250 ($7,315)

B Cadillac DeVille ($7,095)

C Ford Thunderbird ($5,730)

D Mercury Marquis ($5,067)

E Buick LeSabre ($4,567)

F Volvo 144 ($3,590)

G Ford Mustang ($3,132)

H Dodge Dart ($2,665)

I Chevrolet Vega ($2,382)

J VW Beetle ($1,999)

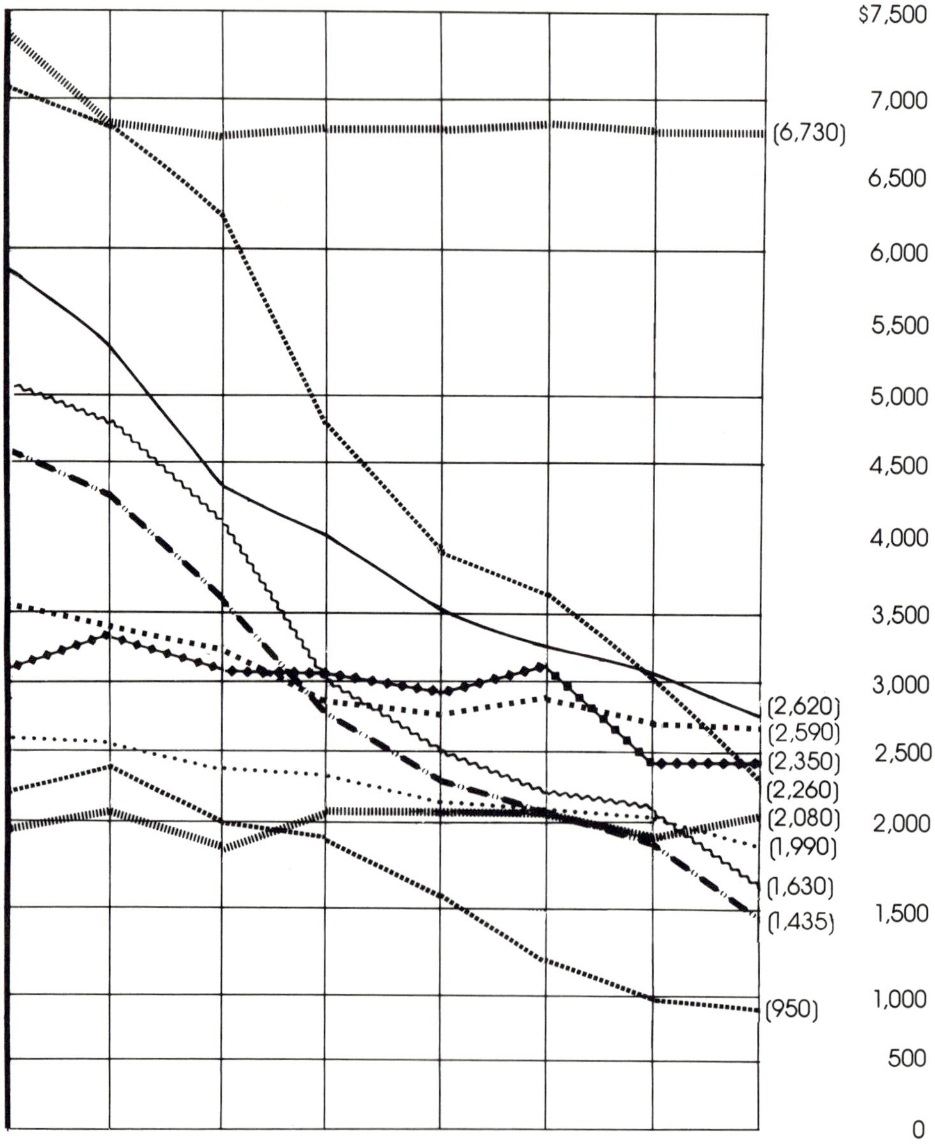

(6,730)
(2,620)
(2,590)
(2,350)
(2,260)
(2,080)
(1,990)
(1,630)
(1,435)
(950)

$7,500
7,000
6,500
6,000
5,500
5,000
4,500
4,000
3,500
3,000
2,500
2,000
1,500
1,000
500
0

*Figures based on Kelley Blue Book's retail values for these models.

Table 4.3 Maintenance/Depreciation — Subcompact Cars*

1st year 2nd year 3rd year 4th year 5th year 6th year 7th year 8th year 9th year 10th year Ten-year Average

$1,200
1,100
1,000
900
800
700
600
500
400
300
200
100
0

Maintenance: ···$390

Depreciation: — $319

*Tables 4.3, 4.4, and 4.5 are based on data contained in "Cost of Owning and Operating an Automobile (1976)" by L. L. Liston and C. A. Aiken, published by the U.S. Department of Transportation, Federal Highway Administration.

**Depreciation is based on estimates of the loss of value of the car in terms of its resale worth.

***Maintenance includes routine maintenance, replacement of minor parts, and major repairs, as well as replacement tires, and accessories. It does *not* include gasoline, oil, insurance, or taxes.

Table 4.4 Maintenance/Depreciation—Compact Cars

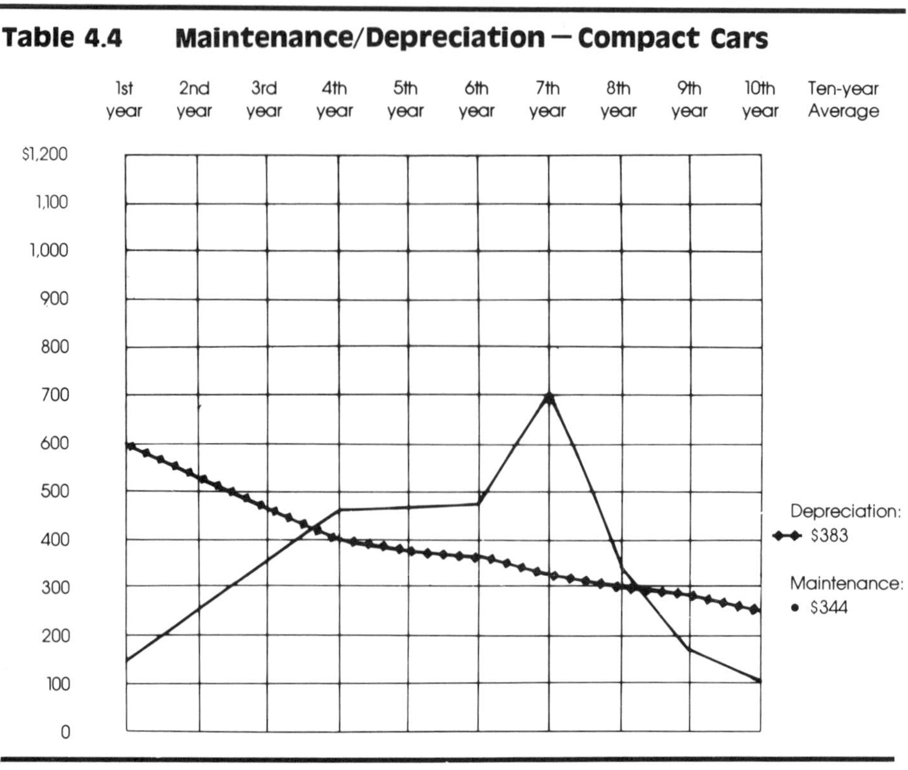

Table 4.5 Maintenance/Depreciation—Standard Cars

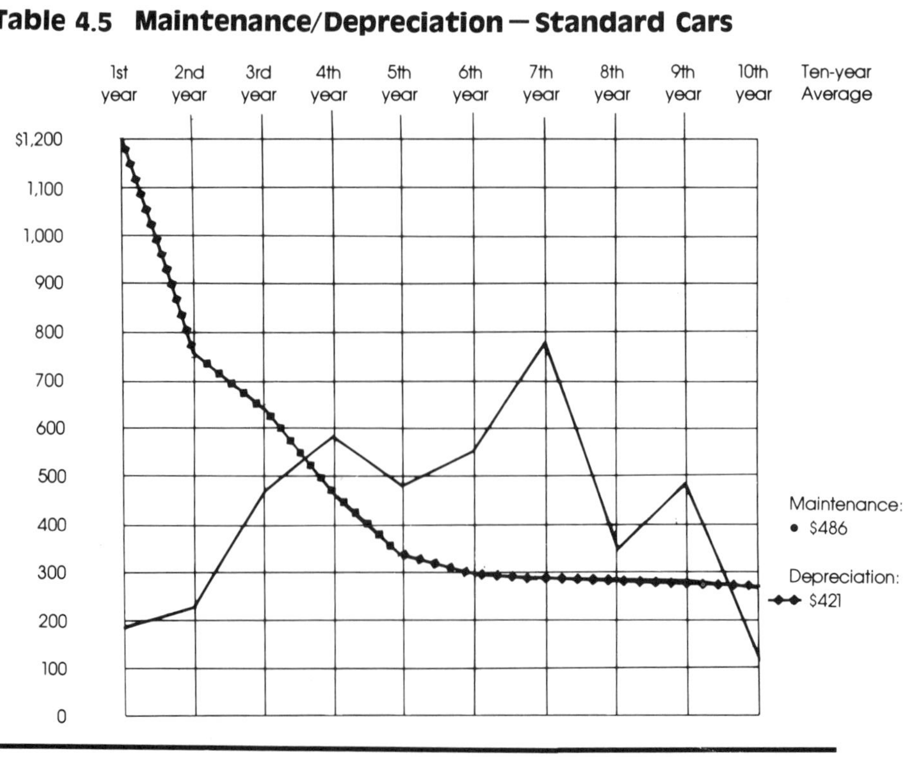

5 Deciding on a car you'd LOVE

Now that you've selected a car-hunting strategy, you'll have to sit down and decide what kind of car you need, want, and can afford.

It's best to do some of this thinking before you hit the used car lots. There are plenty of car hustlers out there who are experts at convincing you that they know what you want even better than you do. Equally important, you'll save yourself a lot of time and unneeded hassle if you know what you're looking for *before* you start running around to car lots.

Let's start with some basic definitions about car types. Later in the chapter, we'll talk more specifically about how to select certain models and what resources are available to differentiate between the cherries and lemons out there on the market.

CAR SIZE

In the past few years, the public and the federal government have forced Detroit to scale down their cars. To meet the federal laws of getting their average fleet mileage up to 27.5 mpg by 1985, Detroit is making substantially smaller cars. Just five years ago, a typical standard-sized car, such as the Chevrolet Impala, weighed about 4,500 pounds and had a wheelbase length (the distance between the front and rear axles) of 122 inches. The '80 model Chevy Impala weighed about a thousand pounds less (about 3,500 pounds) and at 116 inches was a half-foot shorter in wheelbase length.

The other factor is, of course, the competition Detroit is feeling from the smaller, higher gas mileage foreign imports because of the energy crunch. Between April 1978 and April 1979, for instance, imports went from 17 percent of the U.S. market to more than 22 percent. Meanwhile, the sale of smaller cars has increased markedly so that by mid-1979, 53 percent of the sales of American-made cars were either subcompacts or compacts.

Because of this trend, it now makes sense to talk of only three sizes of newer model cars — subcompacts, compacts and big cars. The easiest way to define the differences between those sizes is to compare their wheelbase lengths. A subcompact has a wheelbase length of less than 100 inches; a compact, 101 to 110 inches; and big cars, more than 111 inches.

Because you may be considering cars older than the 1977 or newer models, however, here is a list of the four categories most frequently used by those involved in the car business:

1. *Subcompacts*: Wheelbase less than 101 inches: Ford Pinto, Chevy Vega and Monza, Dodge Colt, AMC Gremlin, VW Beetle, Toyota Corolla and Corona, Datsun B-210 and 510, and so forth.

2. *Compacts*: Wheelbase 102 to 111 inches: Chevrolet Nova, Dodge Dart, Ford Maverick, Buick Apollo, Mercury Comet, Volvo 244, and so forth.

3. *Intermediate (mid-sized)*: Wheelbase 112 to 118 inches: Ford Torino, Chevrolet Malibu and Chevelle, Plymouth Fury, Pontiac Le Mans, and so forth.

4. *Standard (full-sized)*: Wheelbase 119 inches and up: Plymouth, Ford LTD, Chevrolet Impala, Oldsmobile Delta 88 and 98, and so forth. Also included in the standard group are "personal luxury" (or specialty) cars, such as Thunderbird and Buick Riviera, and "luxury" cars, such as Lincoln, Cadillac and Chrysler Imperial.

THE COMFORT VERSUS ECONOMY TRADE-OFF

No one has yet figured out how to build a cheap car that costs very little to maintain *and* provides maximum driving comfort. A Cadillac DeVille may deliver the smoothest and roomiest ride on the road, but it costs a lot more to maintain than a cramped though inexpensive VW Beetle. So you should always expect to give up some driving comfort if you want the most economical car for your money, all other factors (such as age and mileage of the cars) being equivalent.

It is possible, however, to buy an older full-sized American car for less than newer compact or subcompact models. (See depreciation charts in Chapter 4.) But again, you have to sacrifice age and possible higher maintenance costs to obtain comfort.

One rule of thumb to keep in mind: *You should buy the smallest-sized car that meets most of your driving requirements*. If you are a single person who rarely carries passengers or cargo in your car, you are probably wasting your money to buy a full-sized Buick or Ford or a big station wagon. Not only do larger cars usually use more gas, they often cost more to repair.

Remember, though, that no generalization about cars is universally true. Car parts for larger American cars are generally much cheaper and more available than parts for many subcompact foreign-made cars (except VWs and to some extent Toyotas and Datsuns). Therefore, repairs for many of these larger cars are cheaper even though the operating costs may be higher.

BODY STYLES

Not only do you have to have some idea of what size car you want, but you should also think about what body style would best suit you. Here are some pluses and minuses of the various types of cars:

Two-Door versus Four-Door Most of the styles listed below come in two-door and four-door models. If you carry more than one passenger frequently, you'd probably be doing them a service to try to get the four-door variety.

I personally can't stand riding in the back seat of a two-door car, especially in subcompacts. There may not be any more leg room in a four-door model, but I just feel less claustrophobic knowing I can bail out on my own. Besides, I've spent countless frustrating minutes trying to figure out how to extricate myself from the back seat of VW Beetles! Another barb I have to throw at two-door cars: Their doors are somewhat wider than those on a four-door, meaning a two-door can be harder to get in a tight parking space.

My friend Beverly disagrees with my assessment of two-door cars. She thinks four-door cars look too stodgy. Beverly also has two small children, and she prefers being able to put them into the back seat of her coupe (another word for a two-door car) and not have to worry about them opening a door accidentally. She contends, as well, that older two-door cars squeak and rattle less than their four-door counterparts.

Sedans and Hardtops A hardtop car has a metal roof like a sedan, but it does not have a metal pillar behind the front door connecting the roof and the

rest of the car's body. Therefore, when you put the windows down in a hardtop, you have an unobstructed view out of the sides of the car.

Hardtops tend to cost more than sedans of the same model and year, but they also maintain a slightly higher resale value. I don't like hardtops because in case the car ever overturned the absence of that pillar could mean the difference between a hard knock on the head and a crushed skull. But then again, hardtops are nice machines to drive on hot, sunny days with the windows down and the radio blaring away.

The less common pillared hardtop is a cross between the two, with a thin metal pillar between the front and rear windows but without the metal extensions of the front doors (and also of the rear doors in the four-door models).

Station Wagons and Hatchbacks Don't be surprised if in less than a decade the relatively new hatchback style replaces the four-door sedan as the "Great American Car." Hatchbacks combine some features of station wagons and sedans as well as features of the smaller, economy-sized subcompact models.

Both hatchbacks and station wagons have a flat space in the rear for storage of luggage or cargo. While the station wagon typically has a level area

"An Impractical but Wonderful Car."

Attorney Richard Mazer doesn't claim that his '65 Ferrari GTB 275 is a practical car to drive to the office every day. He admits, "Its twelve-cylinder engine isn't very economical at only eight to ten miles per gallon of city driving."

"Because of its big engine," Mazer adds, "It sounds like a real beast going down a city street." To make matters worse, it is hard to handle at low city speeds. "The Ferrari does not get happy until it is going eighty, ninety, or a hundred miles per hour." Which is a problem since Mazer cannot make his car "happy" legally, except at a racing track. Though he has driven his Ferrari at speeds up to 160 mph, Mazer didn't say where he was driving it at the time.

Perhaps in spite of itself, the Ferrari has one useful function. "It's good for clients," Mazer reports. "They think I know what I'm doing when they see what I drive to work."

Mazer bought his car when it was ten years old from a Ferrari dealership for $20,000, which is about $6,000 more than what it cost when it was first manufactured. He says the dealer wasn't willing to bargain over the price. "I guess he figured he'd sit on it until some fool, like me, came in and handed him what he was asking for the car."

But Mazer isn't worried about depreciation: "Somebody is always stopping me on the street these days and offering me thirty or forty thousand for it."

behind the rear seat, the rear seat of a hatchback folds down to provide a similar effect.

I don't like either style because I like to have a locked trunk in which to carry my miscellaneous car tools and occasionally my typewriter and portable tape recorder. Since I've always lived in big cities, I don't like to leave any valuables within sight of the thieves who roam the streets. I've had three different cars broken into while living in Philadelphia, New York City, and San Francisco. But I haven't yet had anything pilfered from a locked car trunk. To get around this problem, some station wagons and some newer models of hatchbacks (such as the more expensive VW Rabbit) have places where you can hide tools or other materials in the rear of the car.

Convertibles, Sports Cars, Vans, and Light Trucks These styles speak for themselves, as you probably know if you're interested in one of them. You should shop for them as you would for any other kind of used car.

Stick versus Automatic Cars with manual transmissions (stick shifts) tend to be somewhat cheaper than those with automatic or semi-automtic transmissions. Sticks also normally give slightly higher gas mileage (one to four mpg) than automatics, though that is not always the case.

Despite the added cost, many people simply prefer the convenience of an automatic transmission, and others may simply never have learned how to drive a manual. I have friends in San Francisco who prefer not having to hassle with a clutch in stop-and-go traffic on steep hills, though I would rather use the clutch than listen to an automatic waste gas as it travels up some of the city's cliff-like streets.

Four, Six, Eight . . .

As with the size of automobiles, there's normally a trade-off between economy and power when you pick cars with larger engines and/or more cylinders. A '79 Honda Civic, with its 76-cubic-inch, four-cylinder engine, probably couldn't beat a '79 Corvette, with a 350-cubic-inch V-8 engine, in a mile race even if you gave the Honda a quarter-mile head start. On the other hand, the Corvette only gets 13 mpg while the Honda's EPA mileage estimate is 28 mpg.

Options

Car makers have shown themselves willing to provide something for everybody. Beyond the standard options like air conditioning, radios, and tinted glass, you can get cars that have TV sets, refrigerators and hot plates — all the conveniences of home. Rather than explain the pluses and minuses of various options, I've provided a checklist of standard options you may want to consider when buying a used car (Table 5.1).

Makes and Models

Let's say you've decided you want a second-hand compact, two-door sedan with automatic transmission, preferably with air conditioning and an FM radio. You still have to figure out what make (car manufacturer) and model to get.

To give you some idea of how large the field is, I counted a total of ninety-seven different makes and models listed in one consumer publication's survey of the new cars of 1979. That's only the beginning since most models come in a variety of body styles. For instance, Ford produces its Pinto model as a two-door Pinto Pony sedan, a two-door sedan, a three-door Pinto Runabout (hatchback), a two-door wagon, and a two-door wagon with a Pinto Squire option — a total of five different body styles. In addition, most of these Pintos can be purchased with a six-cylinder rather than a four-cylinder engine.

Since makes and models can vary considerably from year to year — for example, the '75 Rabbit is substantially different from the '78 VW Rabbit in terms of mechanical reliability — it may seem like an impossible task to keep track of the thousands of alternatives.

But don't despair. You've already narrowed the field considerably once you've made some initial decisions about what size-style-option specifications you're looking for.

There's another reason not to get too overwhelmed by the immense field of auto makes and models out there. It's simply that there are very few models that are absolute lemons. In fact, almost any car produced by a major auto manu-

Table 5.1 Options Checklist

Car Size	*Essential*	*Prefer*	*Maybe*	*No*
Subcompact				
Compact				
Intermediate				
Standard				
Other:				
Body Style				
Sedan, 2-door				
Sedan, 4-door				
Hardtop, 2-door				
Hardtop, 4-door				
Hatchback				
Station Wagon				
Convertible				
Van				
Sports Car				
Light Truck				
Other:				
Transmission				
Manual (stick)				
Automatic				
Engine				
4-cylinder				
6-cylinder				
V-8				
Seats				
Bench in front & rear				
Buckets, front; Bench, rear				
Reclining Seats				
Vinyl Upholstery				
Cloth Upholstery				
Leather Upholstery				

Power Features	*Essential*	*Prefer*	*Maybe*	*No*
Power Steering				
Power Brakes				
Power Front Seat				
Power Windows, Locks				
Audio Options				
AM Radio				
AM/FM Radio				
Stereo Tape Deck				
Rear-seat Speakers				
Other Options				
Air Conditioning				
Tinted Glass				
Sunroof				
Rear-window Defogger				
Clock				
Luggage Rack				
Trailer-towing				

Car Colors

Exterior,

First choice:

Acceptable:

Unacceptable:

Interior,

First choice:

Acceptable:

Unacceptable:

Makes and Models

First choice:

Second choice:

Third choice:

Acceptable:

Unacceptable:

facturer has a reasonable chance of lasting ten years and 100,000 miles, if properly maintained.

By amassing information about various makes and models you are involved in a subtle process of discovering the weak points of various cars. Some cars, such as many Datsun models, tend to have weak clutches. Others, such as VW Beetles, often have lousy heaters. Or still others, such as some Dodge and Plymouth models, frequently have weak starters. These bits of information are good to know in advance of buying a car. They're items you should ask the owners about or have your own mechanic check out (see Chapter 8, "Spotting Lemons").

Above all, don't think that because a car model is what most car buffs would rate as "cherry" every single car of that type will be trouble-free. Each used car is unique. Owners of superbly made cars have abused and mistreated their vehicles to the point that they're worse buys than a lemon-like Chevy Vega.

One final point: You're usually in a better position as a used car buyer if you don't narrow your selection to one specific model. You can, for instance, go through the process of test driving cars, asking friends, mechanics, and others about cars, and spend days in your local library pouring through various consumer publications. After all that work, you may decide you want a subcompact, four-door, 1976 Dodge Colt sedan with manual transmission. After thus narrowing the field, you may quickly discover that you can't find one that meets your specifications, or you may have to wait for a year-and-a-half before one becomes available in your area, or when you do find one, you're totally at the mercy of the seller and you won't be able to bargain to get the best deal on price possible, or, even worse, the one car you've found is in lousy shape when you assumed it ought to be a cherry.

The moral: *Try to select as many acceptable makes and models as possible before starting your car-hunting*. This is a more realistic approach and will make the process of finding a car much easier in the long run.

With that said, here are some pointers on distinguishing among the various makes and models:

Test Drive Nothing beats sitting behind the wheel of a model you are considering purchasing. If you've concluded you want to buy a compact, two-door station wagon but can't decide what make and model would be best, you might find it worthwhile driving a few cars that meet your initial specifications.

Most new car dealerships expect people who are "just looking" to come in and ask to test drive their cars. You can do the same with most used car dealers. No strings attached; it's an accepted part of the business.

Ask the Person Who Owns One If you're interested in how a car runs, nobody is more likely to be honest with you about its pluses and minuses than someone who owns one (provided he or she isn't trying to sell it to you). Ask people you see driving the kind of car you're interested in about its performance, comfort, and so on. Most people are more than willing to talk about their cars.

Ask Your Mechanic If you currently have a car, you probably use one or more mechanics. Since they're in the business of cars, most of them have developed prejudices about different kinds of cars.

My friend Peter was in a hurry to get a used car since his old car was about to give out and was firing on only about four of its eight cylinders. He heard of a '75 Vega he could get for $800, which seemed like a good deal to him. But after asking his mechanic and two other independent garage mechanics whose names he got from the Yellow Pages, Peter decided he'd better pass up the deal.

Kiplinger's *Changing Times* magazine recently published a long article about preferred makes and models of used cars based on its survey of 126 master mechanics. Their top choices were: Subcompacts: Ford Pinto, Chevrolet Chevette, Datsun B-210; Compacts: Dodge Dart, Chevrolet Nova, Ford Maverick; Intermediate: Oldsmobile Cutlass, Chevrolet Malibu, Ford Torino, Buick Century; Standard: Chevrolet Caprice and Impala, Ford LTD, Oldsmobile 88 and 98; Luxury: Lincoln Continental, Cadillac deVille.

Written Resources

There are at least a dozen periodicals and books on the market that purport to give you information about various makes and models of cars. I'd recommend three publications produced by Consumers Union and one publication produced by Consumer Guide as having the best information for the average used car buyer. I have not included some of the auto magazines, such as *Motor Trend* and *Car & Driver*. Although the technical information contained in their analyses of various cars is often quite good, I don't think those kinds of publications are sufficiently harsh in their criticisms of various makes and models. One possible reason is that the publications are supported, in part, by ads from auto manufacturers.

1 Consumers Union produces three publications a year related to used cars. The first is the April issue of its monthly magazine, *Consumer Reports* ($1 per issue or $11 per year), which contains "frequency-of-repair records" for cars from one to six years old. This issue also normally contains a listing of recent used cars that *Consumer Reports* recommends and those it suggests avoiding.

Secondly, Consumer's Union publishes an annual Buying Guide Issue ($3), released in December and sold as a paperback book, which repeats the "frequency-of-repair records" and the CU's choices for good used cars.

Thirdly, CU puts out a *Guide to Used Cars* ($5.50 plus 50¢ postage). This paperback booklet reprints articles that previously appeared in *Consumer Reports* magazine about various models as new cars. It also reprints the April issue's "frequency-of-repair records." This book adds little beyond what is in the April issue or the December Buying Guide Issue, and it is superfluous for regular subscribers to the magazine.

CU's "frequency-of-repair records" are based on questionnaires sent in by more than 250,000 *Consumer Reports* subscribers/car owners. They report on whether they have experienced problems in the previous year in any of eighteen different categories of auto difficulties, from the body and brakes to the engine and transmission.

The "frequency-of-repair records" chart is useful, but as CU does not explain specifically what it means by the term "average" or tell how many cars of a specific model were involved in the survey, the chart shouldn't be treated as the last word on a car's mechanical reliability. For instance, the April 1978 issue of *Consumer Reports* recommended the 1976 Honda Accord as one of the best used cars on the market, and its "frequency-of-repair record" gave a "better than average" rating for its "engine mechanical" category (rings, pistons, cylinders, bearings, camshaft, and oil leaks). Imagine how people who bought 1976 Honda Accords based on the recommendation must have felt when they opened the April 1979 issue and discovered that not only was their model not on the "good bets" list, but its "engine mechanical" rating was "much worse than average."

The *Consumer Reports* ratings worked in the opposite direction, too. The April 1978 issue gave the '76 Corvette a much worse than average rating for its "body exterior," but in April 1979 concluded its "body exterior" was "much better than average" in terms of paint and "average" in terms of rust.

The *Consumer Reports* ratings also have the drawback that they do not include comments from car owners who buy their cars as second-hand or third-hand vehicles. Only the original owners respond to the survey, leaving out many vehicles that are sold within five years.

Despite its shortcomings, *Consumer Reports* gives its readers consistently good information about makes and models of new and used cars. You can order their publications from *Consumer Reports*, P.O. Box 1000, Orangeburg, New York 10962, or buy them at many newsstands and bookstores.

2 *Consumer Guide's Complete Guide to Used Cars*, published each May as a paperback ($2.50), gives a readable summary of the pluses and minuses of dozens of used cars produced within the last decade by both domestic and foreign manufacturers. The book also contains a list of the retail price range of most used cars, though I think other publications are better (see Chapter 9, "The Art of Haggling"). Unlike *Consumers Guide's Annual Guide to New Cars*, which I find altogether too promotional and not nearly critical

Car Salesman John Skeer

enough for the wary car buyer, their used car guide writers aren't afraid to call a lemon a lemon. An example from their 1978 edition: "Chevrolet people got so tired of apologizing for the Vega's dismal failures, so the car was canceled in 1978. But many irate owners say the cancellation came seven years too late."

If you delight in reading through charts and semi-scientific analyses of cars, stick with *Consumer Reports*. But if you prefer a more laid back and chatty discussion about used car models, it's *Consumer Guide*'s book.

Consumer Guide's paperback on used cars is distributed by New American Library and is sold on newsstands throughout the country. Or you can order it directly from *Consumer Guide*, 3841 W. Oakton Street, Skokie, Illinois 60076 (add 75¢ postage).

Final Pointers about Makes and Models

Don't overestimate the value of what you can learn about a specific used car as a result of reading a few books or magazine articles. The ideal car model has yet to be manufactured. Don't ever forget that you are buying a *used* vehicle, and you should assume that its former owner would still be driving it if it were flawless.

More important, a used car's current mechanical condition is related largely to how its former owner drove and maintained it as well as to the quality of care it received from the mechanics who have worked on it. An abusive driver can cause immeasurable damage to the best-made car. That is why I strongly suggest that before you buy a used car, you should have a professional mechanic inspect it (see Chapter 8, "Spotting Lemons").

Part of the reason I do not have a list of preferred used car models in this book is that I think it is misleading to put too much stock in such ratings. Most used car professionals I have interviewed (dealers, salesmen, wholesalers, mechanics) have a much more relaxed attitude about various car models than many nonprofessionals. Not that they do not willingly pass value judgments about different models of used cars. But the people who have been in the business a long time seem to share an attitude that almost any type of used car can provide good transportation for some people. It all depends on what you are looking for in a car.

In fact, I have found it difficult to get a lengthy list of car models which these professionals agree to classify as lemons. For instance, one car wholesaler I interviewed has been buying and selling cars for twenty-five years at the rate of about 100 cars a month (that's more than 30,000 cars!). Before he became a wholesaler, he worked as a professional auto mechanic. The only two car models he would classify as lemons are the Chevrolet Vega (pre-'75) and the Mazda models with rotary engines. He did not mean to imply that he thought all other models were equally good – simply certain models are better for some purposes than others. To him, individual used cars vary so greatly in terms of their condition that it is difficult to make blanket judgments based on make and model.

I would add a few other cars to my lemon list: the older Ford Pintos (not station wagon models) because of the fire danger from being rear-ended, as pointed out in *Mother Jones* magazine in 1977 and subsequent lawsuits against Ford; and the Chevrolet Corvair, based on Ralph Nader's research. I would also be reluctant to buy a VW Beetle based on Nader's criticism of its lack of safety features.

Finally, when you consider maintenance costs of a used car, *remember that the more cars of a particular model that are on the road, the easier it is to get parts* – and generally the less expensive the car is to maintain as it gets older. That is one factor which makes American Motors cars generally less desirable as used cars than those produced by the Big Three (GM, Ford, Chrysler). Similarly, it is why Italian, French, and English cars are often less easy to maintain and repair than many German and Japanese models.

6 Putting the BREAD together

Before you even pick up the newspaper classifieds, you should stop to consider how much you can afford to spend on a used car. Not just to buy it, but all of your costs.

The Hertz Corporation recently conducted a survey which revealed that more than a fourth of the typical American's personal income is soaked up by the costs of owning and operating their automobiles. That's $2,027 per person (or 25.9 percent of the average national per capita income of $7,821).

Just because the average American is spending a quarter of his or her income on cars doesn't mean you should expect to spend the same amount. Most people would probably say they are spending too much of their income on their gas guzzlers. Many of us acknowledge that we spend excessively for our cars and in the same breath we also say we don't know exactly why it costs so much to own and drive a car. "It just adds up," we say.

If you're considering borrowing money to get a loan for a used car, you should make every effort to get the best possible deal. Car loan payments are probably the worst culprits of the "it just adds up" quandry. The money you spend on a car loan usually equals what the car costs you in terms of vehicle depreciation. According to the Hertz study, vehicle depreciation accounted for more than 25 percent of the total ownership and operating costs and was the single largest expense for most car owners.

What's more, car loan payments add up even if you don't ever drive the car. With car insurance, your *monthly loan payments* constitute one of the fixed costs of owning a car. So if you're trying to determine the top price you can pay for a used car, you should have clearly in mind the maximum limit you can afford for your car's monthly loan payments. Those payments don't decrease over time.

At the end of this chapter is a chart you can use to calculate your monthly car expenses (Table 6.4). But before you fill it out, you should consider the question of a down payment and also the various loan options for used cars.

DOWN PAYMENT

Before discussing your various loan options, you should remember that you're normally expected to pay a *down payment* even if you borrow most of the money to pay for the car. In general, you'll be expected to pay a larger down payment for an older used car than for a newer one; and, as we shall discuss below, you often can't borrow for a car that's older than six or seven years. For newer cars, you'll usually be required to pay at least 10 percent down; for older ones, up to 40 percent or even 50 percent. When you're considering how much money to put down on a car, remember that the more you put down, the smaller your monthly payments and the smaller the total interest you'll pay on your debt. In other words, *pay as large a down payment as possible for a used car*.

If you have a car now, it is worth something in case you want to sell it or trade it in. In fact, your current car may be worth enough by itself to cover a down payment on another used car. Usually it's to your advantage to sell your own car privately rather than to trade it in to a dealer. (More on that subject in later chapters.) Regardless, your current car should be worth enough to at least reduce the total amount you have to borrow, if not cover the entire down payment.

One piece of advice to keep in mind is: *Borrow as little money as you can and pay it off in the shortest possible time period*. The more money you borrow, the greater your monthly payments and the longer you will be in debt; and the more time you take to pay off the loan, the greater your total interest costs.

To see how drastically the term or duration of a loan affects the total amount of interest you have to pay, take a look at the total interest cost (TI) column of the auto loan costs chart (Table 6.1). In general, given the same loan amount and interest rate, you have to pay twice as much for a two-year loan as for a one-year loan; three times as much for a three-year loan as for a one-year loan; and four times more for a four-year loan.

(Note: Two factors – inflation and the fact you can deduct interest charges on your income tax return – help to offset the higher total interest costs of a longer term loan.)

Besides the loan term, a higher interest rate on your loan (normally expressed in terms of its Annual Percentage Rate or APR) also increases your total interest cost (TI). Looking at Table 6.1 again, you can see that a two-year loan of $2,000 at 5 percent APR costs $16 a month less than the same loan at 22.5 percent APR – with a total interest cost difference of $396!

Where you get your loan normally determines how great the interest rate will be. Because it can have such a significant impact on your monthly payments and total interest cost, you should consider various options before making a final decision as to where to borrow money. I've listed the seven major options for those interested in used car loans below from the most desirable to the least. You should make every effort to qualify for the cheaper ones, though obviously not everyone has enough money to engage in "self-borrowing" or to take out a passbook savings loan.

In addition to studying the different loan options, you should shop around. Interest rates and loan agreements vary widely, especially those offered by banks and auto dealers. Table 6.2 illustrates how much can be saved by using a cheaper loan option. The chart is based on the interest rates I obtained from seven different financial institutions when I inquired about financing a $2,000 loan to buy a three-year-old Ford Maverick that was selling for $3,200. (Note the impact of the loan term on the total interest cost in Table 6.2. For instance, a three-year credit union loan at 13 percent APR costs nearly as much in total interest as a two-year dealer-financed loan at the much higher 19.75 percent APR – though the monthly payments are obviously much greater for the shorter-term loan.)

LOAN OPTIONS FOR USED CARS

Self-borrowing

Let's say you want to buy a $2,000 car, and you have $2,000 in a savings account that you do not need for the proverbial rainy day. You could decide to pay for the vehicle from the money in your savings account and then repay the account with regular monthly installments as if you had taken out a loan from the bank. You could decide, for instance, that you want to repay the loan over a three-year period at an APR of 5.25 percent, which would be $60.17 per month – still substantially lower than any other loan option. (See Table 6.2.)

Of course, you can choose not to pay back the savings account, but then you're simply out the money for good. By paying back the account, you would have both a car and your savings account restored at the end of three years. You could then use the money (and your car) to buy another used car when you are ready for another car.

Life Insurance Loans

If you have what is known as a "whole-life" insurance policy, you may be able to borrow against its cash value from the insurance company at a relatively low interest rate, usually between 5 and 8 percent APR. The cash value of such a policy is based on how much money you've paid in annual insurance premiums, so you're more apt to have a higher cash value the longer you've had such a policy.

This is the route I took when I got my Datsun B-210. I had a small life insurance policy that my grandmother obtained for me when I was quite young and the annual premium rate was low. When I called up the insurance agent, I learned that the policy had a cash value of about $1,750 and that I could borrow that amount at an amazingly low 5 percent APR.

What's more, the only penalty for not paying back the loan is that the outstanding balance is simply deducted from the amount my beneficiaries receive when I die. In other words, if I were to die the day after I took out a $1,750 loan, the insurance company would pay my beneficiaries only $6,250 instead of the full insurance policy value of $8,000. That's not something that I consider much of a loss since I'd rather have the car today than worry about an extra $1,750 somebody would not get when I die.

Since the insurance company can't lose in the deal, it makes no effort to force me to repay the loan. The company left it completely up to me to figure out a loan repayment schedule, and I didn't have to sign any documents agreeing to pay back the money over any period of time at any rate. In my case, I decided to repay it in three years at about $54 a month, but I could just as easily have decided to repay it over a period of one year, ten years, or never. Or I could have repaid it all at once. It was completely up to me.

The obvious hitch is that the insurance company continues to earn 5 percent interest as long as the loan has not been repaid. I calculated that if I didn't pay the loan back at all, I would owe more than $3,000 in interest payments alone by the time I reached age 65. That's more than a thousand dollars more than the original loan. The company would then simply deduct the $3,000 and the $1,750 from the insurance policy of $8,000, leaving my beneficiaries only about $3,000.

It is to my advantage to pay off the loan for another reason. Once it's paid off, I can borrow against the cash value of the policy again. If I pay off the loan in three years, I'll not only have a fully paid for car, but I'll have $1,750 to borrow again to buy another one.

Passbook Loans

If you have a savings account, you might consider borrowing against it to buy a used car. Most banks and savings and loan associations offer what are called passbook loans that use the savings you have on deposit as the collateral for your loan. This method might have appeal if a. you have difficulty getting a loan from another source, since no credit history or reference is normally required for a passbook loan; b. you have savings you have no intention of using during the term of the loan; and c. you want to have the formality of a bank loan to force you to pay back the borrowed money.

For passbook loans, banks and savings and loan associations normally charge between 1 percent and 3 percent above the interest rate they offer for your savings account. In other words, if your savings account is earning 5.5 percent interest, the bank might charge you between 6.5 and 8.5 percent APR for a passbook loan. Since the amount of interest different banks and savings and loan associations charge for passbook loans varies, it pays you to shop around by calling several savings institutions to find the one that charges the least amount for a passbook loan. The other variable to keep in mind is that banks and savings and loan associations typically permit you to only borrow a certain percentage of your savings account as a passbook loan. Often they let you borrow only 90 percent of your savings account.

Here's how it would work if you were borrowing $2,000 as a passbook loan. (You would need to have slightly more than $2,222 in your savings account or savings certificate account to be able to borrow the $2,000 if your bank or savings and loan association only permits you to borrow 90 percent of your account.) Let's say your savings account currently earns 5 percent in interest and the bank's loan officer tells you that the bank charges 2.5 percent above the savings interest rate for passbook loans, or 7.5 percent APR in this case. As you can see from Table 6.1, you would have to pay back the $2,000 at the rate of about $174 a month for a one-year loan; $90 a month for a two-year loan; and $62 a month for a three-year loan.

In the example above, your savings account would still be earning interest at the rate of 5 percent per year, or $100 each year for $2,000 in savings. However, you cannot withdraw money from the savings account until the loan is paid off because you would still be using the savings account as collateral for the loan. (In some cases, a bank will permit you to withdraw an amount equal to what has been paid on the loan. For example, once you have paid $750 of a $2,000 loan, the bank may allow you to withdraw up to $750. But you would still need to keep at least $1,250 in the account as collateral.)

Because you are still earning interest on the savings account, you may think the loan is costing you only the 2.5 percent difference between the savings account and loan interest rates. But the two are entirely separate forms of interest rates, and you will only get confused by trying to compare them with each other. Remember that the passbook savings loan costs you 7.5 percent APR in interest because you would have earned the money from the savings account had you not borrowed money for the car. It's better to consider the savings account merely as the collateral you used for the passbook loan.

Credit Union Loans

If you belong to a credit union, you can probably get a loan at a smaller interest rate than at a commercial bank. Some credit unions also will loan money for cars that are somewhat older than those for which banks will lend. For instance, the California State Employees Credit Union offers its members the rate of 12 percent for loans on new cars or those less than two years old. That credit union also offers loans at 13 percent on cars three years old or more (though it won't provide loans for cars not listed in the Blue Book).

If you don't belong to a credit union, you might find it worthwhile to try to find one you could join. While most credit unions are related to employment, there are others that have other rules for membership. For instance, some consumer co-op stores have affiliated credit unions that you can join once you've joined the co-op. This route is rarely one you should count on if you need to borrow money quickly. Credit unions usually have rules about belonging for a certain period of time before you can borrow money.

Commercial Bank Loans

If you decide to try for a bank loan for your car, plan to spend some time shopping around. A few phone calls can save you a lot of money and hassle.

Before you begin looking for a used car bank loan, you should be aware that each bank may have its own peculiar rules and regulations about used car loans. For one thing, banks normally charge slightly higher rates for used cars than for new cars on the theory that used cars are a riskier investment from their standpoint. Other variables that you should keep in mind when shopping for a bank loan are:

Age of the Car You don't have to have a specific car in mind when you approach a bank, but you should know the approximate age of the car you are going to buy. The older the car is, the harder it will be to borrow money for it. Many banks simply won't loan money for a car older than two or three years, and virtually none will let you borrow for a car that is older than six years since such cars are no longer listed in the Blue Book.

Maximum Loan Amount If you want to buy a used car, don't expect to be able to borrow the full amount from a bank. When I was looking for a bank loan for my '75 Datsun B-210, I learned that many of the banks would only lend me 80 percent of the "low Blue Book" (wholesale) value of the car. At the time, the wholesale value of the B-210 was $1,825, so I could only have borrowed $1,460. I would have to raise the other thousand dollars (that model retailed for at least $2,500 at the time) to buy the car from some other source. Loaning money on only a percentage of the wholesale used car price is a common banking practice.

Maximum Loan Term In a recent survey of 22 banks in San Francisco, I discovered that twelve would loan money for a used car (costing about $2,000) for no more than 24 months, while four would lend the money for a maximum of 30 months, and only six would let me borrow the money for 36 months. Again, banks view used car loans as risky propositions, so they don't want to let you have the money any longer than absolutely necessary.

Loan Rates As with consumer finance companies, banks will generally offer lower rates (APR) for larger loans, and they will permit such loans to be paid back over a longer period of time. Table 6.3 illustrates how one bank's rates vary according to the size of the loan.

Bank rates vary considerably even in the same locality. In the survey of twenty-two local banks I mentioned earlier, I found a range of 3.5 percent among banks for a $2,000 loan for 36 months. That meant the difference of $3.40 per month in the payments and nearly $125 over a period of 36 months in additional interest costs. Again, a few phone calls are certainly worth $125 to most people.

Preparing to Get a Bank Loan One final word about bank loans before moving along to other options. Bankers are not casual people, mellow about lending money. If you have never obtained a bank loan before and don't have a sterling credit record, make sure you are only asking for an amount of money you can justify to a skeptical loan officer.

I didn't follow this advice when I applied for a used car loan from a local bank where I had a checking account for several years. I initially asked for a loan of $2,500, thinking that I could always reduce my request if I needed less. Never having applied for a bank loan before, I was not prepared for the loan officer's detailed questions about my monthly income and expenses. Ultimately, he agreed to loan me between $1,000 and $1,500 after he checked into my employment and credit background. But it seemed to me that he only granted the loan because I had a checking account with his bank – a factor that tends to work in your favor if your account has had few or no bounced checks.

It would have been much better if I had gone to the bank totally prepared with a written monthly budget indicating my expenses and had only asked for an amount of money whose monthly payments would be clearly within my budget. I had simply not done my homework beforehand and approached it too casually. The same advice applies when you try to get a loan from other lending institutions, such as consumer-finance companies or credit unions.

Inflation and Car Financing.

Most financial advisers counsel prospective car buyers to pay off a car loan as quickly as possible because a longer loan term means higher total interest costs. For instance, a 24-month loan of $3,000 at 15 percent APR costs $491 in interest, while the same loan amount at the identical interest rate for 36 months results in a total interest cost of $744. (See Table 6.1.)

In fact, you could generalize and state that a longer term loan at the same APR would cost more in interest than a shorter term loan. Right?

Not necessarily so, according to a 1977 study by Western Women's Bank. The bank studied the "effective cost" of car loans by taking into account the impact of inflation and of tax savings from the higher interest charges. On the basis of its study, the bank concluded that there was little difference in the "effective cost" between three- and four-year loans of $5,000.

Specifically, the bank charted the "effective cost" of two $5,000 car loans – the first, at 10.14 percent APR for 36 months; the second at the rate of 10.39 percent for 48 months. Without taking inflation or tax deductions into account, the shorter term loan would be more than three hundred dollars cheaper than the 48-month loan ($820 versus $1,132). But when a moderate 6 percent annual inflation rate was deducted, the 36-month loan would save $492 while the 48-month loan would be reduced by $679. In addition, the bank computed the tax deductions a borrower could claim for the interest charges of $246 and $340 respectively for the 36- and 48-month loans. The result: the "effective cost" of the 36-month loan was $82, while the 48-month loan's was $113.

Consumer-Finance Loans

You should place loans from one of the consumer-finance companies – like Household (HFC), General, or Beneficial – in the same last resort category as dealer financing.

Most consumer finance companies don't differentiate between money they lend for a used car and money they lend for any other purpose: they just lend money. So their rates are usually based on the amount of money you borrow and the term of the loan. In many states, these companies are regulated so that there is no difference in the rates between one company, say HFC, and another company, such as Beneficial.

The more money you borrow from consumer finance companies (or from most banks), the lower your APR. For instance, California's consumer finance companies charge 24.9 percent APR for loans of less than $1,500, and 18 percent for loans in excess of that amount. You can also take a longer time to pay back a larger loan from a consumer finance company (the same is true for most banks, too). Again using California's consumer finance companies as an example, you must repay any amount less than $1,500 within 24 months; between $1,500 and $2,500 within 36 months; and more than $2,500 within 48 months.

Since consumer finance companies are similar to banks in that they would normally require you to use the car as collateral for the loan, there is really no advantage to seeking a loan from one of these companies unless you simply can't get a loan from another source.

Auto Finance Counselor Audrey B. Ward

Dealer Financing

If you want to buy a second-hand used car from a new car dealer, the salesman will probably offer to take care of the financing of a loan on the car. He may explain that the dealership has an arrangement with a local bank so that you don't even have to talk to the bank yourself.

When I was looking for a second-hand car several years ago, I found a VW Rabbit that I was interested in buying. The salesman assured me I would qualify for one of their loans through a local bank. But, he admitted, it would cost "a couple of percentage points" more than if I got a loan directly from the same local bank. The reason for the extra few points, according to the salesman, was that the VW dealer assumed some of the risk for the loan. That is, the VW dealership would have to pay if I didn't. What the VW salesman didn't say was that if I defaulted on the loan and the car were repossessed, the dealership would be in a better position than the bank to convert the car to cash.

You should take dealer financing only as a last resort. "A couple of percentage points" adds up to money out of your pocket for a dubious amount of convenience. A local newspaper in San Francisco recently surveyed dealer loans and discovered that they ranged from approximately one percentage point to a full eight percentage points higher than for similar bank loans.

Translate those percentage points into dollars and cents by looking at Table 6.1. For a 36-month $2,000 loan at an APR of 15 percent, you would pay $496 in interest. An APR that is 2.5 percent higher, or 17.5 percent, costs nearly $100 more ($585). For 5 percent more, or 20 percent, you'd spend almost $200 more in interest ($676); and at 7.5 percent more, or 22.5 percent, you'd fork over nearly $300 more ($768). In addition, you'd be paying $8 a month more in your monthly installments ($77 instead of $69) for the 22.5 percent loan than for a 15 percent loan.

Remember: The extra money you spend on higher interest payments doesn't get you a better car. It's just money effectively thrown out the window.

MONTHLY CAR EXPENSES

Once you have determined the most appropriate loan option, you should consider your car loan payments as part of the total picture of your car expenses. Table 6.4 can help you calculate your monthly automobile expenditures. If you are still trying to determine how expensive a car you can afford, you can use Table 6.4 to give you a clearer idea about a feasible monthly loan payment in light of your overall auto budget.

You should first address the question of what is the maximum you can afford to spend on an automobile per month (Table 6.4, line 1). If you already have a car, you can probably make a quick estimate based on your current expenditures. If you are about to buy your first car, remember that the typical American spends about one-fourth of his or her annual income for automobile expenses. That is a sizeable percentage of someone's income for wheels, but at least that should give you some idea of what is commonplace. At any rate, whatever you determine to be the maximum you can spend per month (line 1), make sure the total estimate (line 8) does not exceed that amount.

Before you consider your monthly loan payments, you should try to get an estimate from some auto insurance agents about your annual insurance bill (line 2). If you are unfamiliar with what kind of insurance coverage you need, take a look at the auto insurance section of Chapter 11, "Now that you've bought it. . . ." Once you have obtained the cheapest estimate of your car insurance, divide the annual estimate by twelve for the purposes of Table 6.4, line 2.

An increasingly large chunk of most car owners' budgets is being absorbed by gasoline costs. You can make a quick estimate of the total amount you will spend annually on gasoline if you know your car's gas mileage, the average price per gallon, and how far you expect to drive per year. With those figures, you can turn to Table 12.1 in Chapter 12 and look up the annual fuels costs for your automobile. (Remember that if you drive more or less than 10,000 miles per year to multiply the figure given in Table 12.1 by the appropriate factor. For instance, if you drive 5,000 miles a year, multiply Table 12.1's figures by 0.5; if you drive 12,500 miles annually; multiply by 1.25.) Divide the annual fuel cost estimate from Table 12.1 by twelve before writing it on line 3 of Table 6.4.

Maintenance and repair costs are inherently unpredictable. But any car owner would be remiss not to budget some money for these expenses. Consider yourself lucky if you never have to spend a dime for major repairs on your car. But if you have planned for these costs in advance, you are less likely to feel so devastated financially when they occur to you – as they do from time to time to 99.9 percent of all car owners.

How much you should expect to spend on maintenance and repairs is more difficult to estimate than other car expenses. One method might be to take a look at the annual maintenance and repair costs of the Department of Transportation survey contained in Chapter 4, Tables 4.3, 4.4 and 4.5. To take the example of a four-year-old standard-sized car, consider Table 4.5. According to the DOT survey, car owners reported their maintenance and repair costs to be nearly $600 in the fourth year ($50 per month). That would be a realistic estimate for the purposes of line 4 of Table 6.4 for that kind of vehicle.

Using your estimates for auto insurance, gas, maintenance and repairs, and tolls, parking, garage (line 5), you can add together a subtotal of monthly car expenses (line 6). Next you should subtract the subtotal (line 6) from your upper limit (line 1) to determine the *maximum* amount you can afford to spend on your monthly loan payment (line 7). By adding the subtotal and your monthly loan payment together, you can establish your total monthly car expense estimate (line 8).

YOUR TOP PRICE FOR A CAR

Once you have determined how much you can afford in terms of monthly loan payments, you can figure out how much you can spend for a used car. You should only go out to the used car lots and confront a professional car salesman when you have that figure – your top price – firmly in mind. And do not offer to spend more than that amount. (More on how to bargain for a used car in Chapter 9,"The Art of Haggling.")

Your top price equals your down payment plus your car loan. In terms of the loan, you can easily figure out how large a loan you can obtain once you know what you can afford in terms of your monthly loan payments and have chosen the appropriate loan option for your situation. For instance, if you can afford

Table 6.1 Auto Loan Costs

This table shows the costs (rounded off to the nearest dollar) for auto loans of $500 to $6,000. Both the monthly payment (MP) and the total interest cost (TI) are shown for car loans at Annual Percentage Rates (APR) of 5 to 22.5 percent with loan terms from 12 to 48 months.

Loan	Amount	$500		$1,000		$1,500		$2,000		$2,500		$3,000		$4,000		$5,000		$6,000	
APR	Term	MP	TI	MP	TI	MP	TI	MP	TI	MP	TI	MP	TI	MP	TI	MP	TI	MP	TI
	12 mos.	*43*	14	*86*	27	*128*	41	*171*	55	*214*	68	*257*	82	*342*	109	*428*	136	*514*	164
5%	24 mos.	*22*	27	*44*	53	*66*	80	*88*	106	*110*	133	*132*	159	*175*	212	*219*	265	*263*	318
	36 mos.	*15*	40	*30*	79	*45*	119	*60*	158	*75*	198	*90*	237	*120*	316	*150*	395	*180*	474
	48 mos.	*12*	53	*23*	105	*35*	158	*46*	211	*58*	264	*69*	316	*92*	422	*115*	527	*138*	633
	12 mos.	*43*	21	*87*	41	*130*	62	*174*	82	*217*	103	*260*	123	*347*	164	*434*	205	*521*	247
7.5%	24 mos.	*23*	40	*45*	80	*68*	120	*90*	160	*113*	200	*135*	240	*180*	320	*225*	400	*270*	480
	36 mos.	*16*	60	*31*	120	*47*	180	*62*	240	*78*	300	*93*	360	*124*	479	*156*	599	*187*	719
	48 mos.	*12*	80	*24*	161	*36*	241	*48*	321	*60*	402	*73*	482	*97*	643	*121*	803	*145*	964

between ninety and one hundred dollars a month and you qualify for a commercial bank loan at approximately 17.5 percent APR interest, you could get a two-year loan of $2,000 or a three-year loan of $2,500, according to Table 6.1.

Remember that when you buy a car, you will also have to pay for license fees and sales tax. Your state's Department of Motor Vehicles can tell you how much it will cost you in license fees for your car, and any dealer can give you the same information (if you are buying a car from a dealer). You will also be required to pay the state sales tax (usually the same amount as on other major consumer purchases) whether you are buying the car from a private party or from a dealer. If you buy a car for $2,495 and your state's sales tax is 5.5 percent, you will owe an additional $137 in sales tax.

In addition, most used car buyers usually should expect to spend some money for some initial maintenance and repairs on the car. You should have a good idea whether the car needs any immediate repairs before you purchase the vehicle. And you should plan to sink some money in soon after you buy the car for such minor items as an oil change and lubrication. (See Chapter 11, "Now That You've Bought It . . .") At any rate, you should plan to set aside some money for these initial expenses rather than put your last penny into the car's purchase price.

Table 6.1 Auto Loan Costs

Loan	Amount	$500		$1,000		$1,500		$2,000		$2,500		$3,000		$4,000		$5,000		$6,000	
APR	Term	MP	TI	MP	TI	MP	TI	MP	TI	MP	TI	MP	TI	MP	TI	MP	TI	MP	TI
	12 mos.	44	28	88	55	132	83	176	110	220	138	264	165	352	220	440	275	528	330
10%	24 mos.	23	52	46	108	69	162	92	215	115	269	138	323	185	430	231	538	277	645
	36 mos.	16	81	32	162	48	243	65	323	81	404	97	485	129	647	161	808	194	970
	48 mos.	13	109	25	218	38	327	51	435	63	544	76	652	101	870	127	1087	152	1305
	12 mos.	45	35	89	69	134	104	178	138	223	173	267	207	356	276	445	345	535	414
12.5%	24 mos.	24	68	47	135	71	203	95	271	118	339	142	390	189	542	237	677	284	812
	36 mos.	17	102	33	205	50	307	67	409	84	511	100	613	134	818	167	1022	201	1226
	48 mos.	13	138	27	276	40	414	53	552	66	690	80	828	106	1103	133	1379	159	1655
	12 mos.	45	42	90	83	135	125	181	166	226	208	271	249	361	332	451	416	542	499
15%	24 mos.	24	82	48	164	73	246	97	328	121	410	145	491	194	655	242	819	291	982
	36 mos.	17	124	35	248	52	372	69	496	87	620	104	744	139	992	174	1240	208	1488
	48 mos.	14	168	28	336	42	504	56	672	70	840	84	1008	111	1344	139	1680	167	2016
	12 mos.	46	49	91	97	137	146	183	195	229	243	274	292	366	389	457	487	549	584
17.5%	24 mos.	25	96	50	193	75	289	99	385	124	481	149	577	199	770	248	962	298	1154
	36 mos.	18	147	36	293	54	439	72	585	90	732	108	878	144	1170	180	1463	215	1755
	48 mos.	15	199	29	398	44	597	58	795	73	994	87	1193	116	1590	146	1988	175	2385
	12 mos.	46	56	93	112	139	167	185	223	232	279	278	335	371	446	463	558	556	670
20%	24 mos.	25	111	51	222	76	332	102	443	127	554	153	665	204	886	254	1108	305	1329
	36 mos.	19	169	37	338	56	507	74	676	93	845	112	1014	149	1352	186	1690	223	2028
	48 mos.	15	231	30	461	46	692	61	922	76	1152	91	1382	122	1843	152	2304	183	2764
	12 mos.	47	63	94	126	141	189	188	252	235	315	282	378	375	504	469	630	563	756
22.5%	24 mos.	26	126	52	251	78	377	104	502	130	628	156	753	209	1004	261	1255	313	1506
	36 mos.	19	192	38	384	58	576	77	768	96	961	115	1153	154	1537	192	1921	231	2305
	48 mos.	16	263	32	525	48	788	64	1051	79	1314	95	1576	127	2102	159	2627	191	3152

Table 6.2 Comparison of Auto Loan Options*

Type of loan	APR	24-month loan MP	24-month loan TI	36-month loan MP	36-month loan TI
Self-borrowing	5.25%	$ 87.97	111.28	60.17	166.12
Life insurance	6.50%	89.10	138.40	61.30	206.80
Passbook savings	7.25%	89.78	154.72	61.99	231.64
Credit union	13.00%	95.09	282.16	67.39	426.04
Commercial bank	16.75%	98.65	367.60	71.06	558.16
Consumer finance	18.00%	99.85	396.40	72.31	603.16
Dealer financing	19.75%	101.75	437.20	74.08	666.88

*Based on a $2,000 loan for a three-year-old car from actual quotations from seven specific financial institutions. This table is for comparison purposes only. Interest rates vary widely among institutions of the same category, and they also vary somewhat from state to state. APR is the Annual Percentage Rate; MP is the monthly payment; TI is the total interest cost.

Table 6.3 Bank Loan Rates

This table shows the used car loan rate schedule of the Bank of America, the nation's largest commercial bank, as of December 1979. Bank of America's rates, like those of any other bank, can change slightly from day to day in response to the bank's needs to loan more or less money, competition from other banks, and general market conditions.

Loan amount	*APR*	*Maximum loan term*
$1,999 or less	20.25%	36 mos.
$2,000 to $2,999	16.75%	36 mos.
$3,000 to $3,999	16.50%	48 mos.
$4,000 to $7,999	15.50%	48 mos.
$8,000 or more	14.75%	48 mos.

Table 6.4 Your Monthly Car Expense Estimate*

1. ________ Your upper limit. (The maximum you can afford per month.)
2. ________ Auto insurance.
3. ________ Gas.
4. ________ Maintenance.
5. ________ Tolls, parking, garage.
6. ________ Subtotal. (Add lines 2 through 5.)
7. ________ Monthly loan payment. (Should not exceed your upper limit [line 1] minus the subtotal [line 6]).
8. ________ Total estimated monthly auto expense. (Add lines 6 and 7. Should be less than line 1.)

*See text related to "Monthly car expenses."

7 When and where to BUY your used car

The second-hander should find summer especially suitable for car-hunting. Between July and September, many new car dealerships advertise their special year-end clearance sales on the current year's models. Besides taking advantage of the better deals available on new cars, many Americans may pick the summer as the optimum time to buy a new car because they want newer vehicles for their holiday vacations.

At any rate, many dealerships find themselves with full lots of second-hand cars during the summer months. They usually keep the better trade-in vehicles and sell off the remaining ones – including third-hand cars and clunkers – to wholesalers and used car dealers. That also means that third-handers and clunker mongers can find the greatest selection of cars during the summer months.

Some car salesmen have told me, however, that the summer months aren't necessarily the best time to get the best deal on a used car. They point to the slower months, especially the period of time just before and after the Christmas holidays when many American consumers become afflicted with the empty pocketbook syndrome. With fewer people ready to buy used cars, some salesmen are more anxious to make sales since most get paid strictly on a commission basis.

Regardless of when you choose to do your car hunting, whenever possible you should try to do your shopping on sunny days. A little rain can do temporary wonders to the body surface of even a badly rusted vehicle. It's amazing, too, how many people buy used cars they've only seen at night when bumps, dents and scratches – let alone more serious flaws – are hard to notice. *Never go used car shopping on a rainy evening.*

Buying from a Private Party

The ideal person to buy a used car from is a relative or someone you know well. They are the only ones you can probably trust to give you an accurate history of the vehicle and to be honest with you about why they are getting rid of it. Unfortunately, most relatives or friends don't happen to have a good used car available when you are in the market, or the one they have doesn't fit your needs.

What's even worse, very few of us would not blame the friend or relative for mechanical problems that develop in a car we've bought from them. Almost everyone can tell a used car story about a strained family relationship or broken friendship caused by a lemon. Even though you're on safest grounds buying a car from someone you know or love, don't bother unless you're prepared from the outset that the car might become a lemon. That's worth repeating in capital letters: DON'T BUY A USED CAR FROM A RELATIVE OR FRIEND UNLESS YOU'RE FULLY PREPARED FOR A LEMON. Now you can't say I didn't warn you.

There's no clear-cut advantage to buying a used car from a private owner rather than from a dealer, or visa versa. (For what it's worth, about half of all used cars are sold by private owners.) However, one plus for buying privately is that most private owners aren't selling their cars to make a profit. They're usually out to get as much as they can for their automobile. But car-selling isn't their sole source of income. For that reason, you may be able to get a better bargain than with a professional middleman, provided you are willing to haggle (see Chapter 9, "The Art of Haggling").

At the same time, you can often ascertain the true history of a car from a private owner. Many car dealers intentionally keep their salesmen in the dark about a used car's former owners (see Chapter 10, "Confessions of Used-Car Salesmen"). By contrast, private car owners should be able to tell you exactly how they obtained the car, how they have driven it while they've had it, what repairs or problems it's had while they've owned it, and why they are getting rid of it.

Unfortunately not all people selling cars privately are either legitimate or honest. Anybody who's been around the used car business any length of time knows guys who sell cars as a way of picking up extra cash. (See section on the "Curbstoner" in Chapter 10.) That doesn't mean "curbstoners" don't occasionally sell excellent cars at good prices. But they aren't the typical private party owners you're expecting to meet when answering an ad in your local newspaper. Some used car dealers also pose as private party owners, though this practice is frowned upon by some state law enforcers. And even many legitimate private party owners don't tell you the truth about their own cars. They may be knowingly unloading a lemon, but they talk about it as though it's the greatest car Detroit ever produced.

Remember the bottom line about private auto transactions: There are almost no state or federal laws regulating private sales as opposed to sales by new or used car dealers. So when you discuss buying a car from a private party, *beware of the following situations*:

1. The seller has owned the car only briefly. This could mean that he or she is trying to get rid of it quickly because the car is a mechanical nightmare. Or it could mean the current owner has only bought the car to make a quick buck. You may be dealing with a "curbstoner."
2. The seller doesn't own the car. It could mean the car is stolen or that there's some other fly-by-night scheme involved.
3. You find the seller's story about the history of the car and why it's being sold odd or inconsistent. There must be a reason he or she is hiding something.
4. The seller has no receipts for major repairs he or she claims were performed on the car.
5. The seller cannot produce the proper registration and title papers. If there are any legal complications about the car, the car might be stolen or it might not be fully paid for, in which case a bank or finance institution might be the actual owner. Don't hand over any money until you're totally convinced you will become the sole legal owner.
6. The seller won't permit you to have your mechanic do a thorough check on the car. Even if you don't intend to have a mechanic test it, you should find out whether the owner has any objection to your having it looked at by an expert.

There can, of course, be reasonable explanations for any of the above situations. The seller could have bought the car after arriving in town last week and then find he has to leave town for good as of tomorrow's midnight flight. He also may have misplaced all the car's papers and receipts in the turmoil and feel compelled to sell the car to the first person to offer his selling price. But then again. . . . Only you can be the judge of the veracity and integrity of the seller. You don't have much recourse if you make a mistake.

AVIS
Young
used cars
FOR SALE
877-6763
200
EL CAMINO

Used Rental Cars for Sale.

Before 1970 the major car rental agencies disposed of all of the thousands of used vehicles in their rental fleets through auto wholesalers and wholesale auctions. These companies still wholesale some of their cars (particularly ones with major accident damage), but they have recently jumped with both feet into the lucrative retail used car trade.

In 1978, for instance, Hertz was calling itself the "world's largest retailer of used cars" and sold more than 45,000 cars at 116 retail outlets located throughout the country.

Unlike buying a new or used car from a car dealer or a private party, you cannot bargain over the price at one of these rental lots. In one of its brochures, Hertz writes: "The price tag on the car is the price you pay. So there's no dickering or haggling. It's the business-like way to buy your car." (Of course, Hertz's "business-like way" is good for Hertz's own business since the main beneficiary of the "unbusiness-like" bargaining and haggling is often the customer.)

The rental car companies generally peg their "firm price" near the price being charged by car dealers for similar model cars, that is, the high Blue Book or retail value of the car. When the rental companies advertise a sale of one of their models, the price is frequently several hundred dollars less than the high Blue Book price. In short, the price advertised by most rental companies is comparable to what you would pay for a one- or two-year old used car at a new car dealership.

The rental companies have made a special effort to combat two obvious problems many potential customers perceive with purchasing a used rental car – the fact the car has had many previous drivers and its excessive mileage (twenty to thirty thousand miles on a one-year-old automobile is common). These companies offer their customers a "limited warranty." According to Avis's John Mannina (see photo), Avis's "limited power train warranty" covers "only the engine and transmission" for a period of twelve months or twelve thousand miles, whichever comes first. (In other words, the warranty does *not* cover the brakes, electrical accessories, and so forth. In this respect, the rental companies' warranties are quite different from the typical new car warranty.)

You have a somewhat better chance of challenging an unfair practice by a new or used car dealer. But in most cases, your chances of winning a case against a dealer are not great enough that you should stay away from private party deals for that reason alone.

Dealers have one obvious plus – you can see many cars at once. Most used car lots, even ones operated by new car dealers, have cars from a variety of manufacturers. Another advantage of buying from some dealers: Many offer limited warranties, though you have to be careful to read the small print of these contracts (see Chapter 9).

Both private parties and car dealers commonly use the newspaper classifieds to advertise used cars. By the time you pick up the classifieds for serious car-hunting, you should have a good idea of what kind of car you want to buy (makes, models, body styles) and what price range you can afford. Table 13.1 at the end of the book provides a glossary of common terms used in newspaper want-ads to help you decipher the jargon.

One word of advice: Stay clear of cars that are advertised as needing work, as a mechanic's special, or some equivalent phrase. Unless you are a professional mechanic, it is highly unlikely that such cars are worth the investment — even if it looks like a genuine bargain! This is especially true of older cars since parts are often difficult to obtain.

Used Cars from New Car Dealers or Independents

Second-handers have little choice since most second-hand cars are sold privately or by new car dealers who've obtained the cars as trade-ins. By the same token, most third-hand cars and clunkers wind up on independent used car lots or are sold privately. So the decision about where to buy your used car is largely one you've already made by the time you've picked your car-hunting strategy.

However, here are some general points to remember. Although new car dealers typically sell the best of their trade-in vehicles, that isn't necessarily true. Some of these dealers also get cars that were formerly fleet vehicles — such as former police cars that have been driven hard — or rented cars. Look carefully at plain-colored, four-door sedans for tell-tale bore holes where sirens or radios may have once been located. You might notice unusual paint splotches on the front doors where police or government symbols may have been painted over. The moral: Don't assume that a car is a genuine one-owner vehicle just because it's sitting on a new car dealer's used car lot.

Finally, anyone looking for a good second-hand car should pay particular attention to the "glitter lots" — the name given used car lots located in wealthier neighborhoods or suburbs of major metropolitan areas. In those places, many of the drivers have the bucks to maintain their cars well, so they trade-in vehicles that are often in top shape. Because the demand for new cars in these communities often far exceeds that for used cars, the new car dealerships are sometimes overstocked with high quality used cars. Just because these dealerships are located in ritzy areas doesn't mean the price for their cars is any higher than in the middle-income neighborhoods. On the contrary, you may be able to strike an even better deal by shopping around in such lots.

Used Rent-a-Car Lots

The big four car rental agencies (Avis, Budget, Hertz, and National), as well as some of the smaller regional ones, run their own used car lots. In fact, Hertz claims to sell more used cars every year than any other company.

Most rental agencies offer some kind of extended warranty with their cars. Hertz and Avis, for example, offer a limited power train warranty of 12,000 miles or twelve months, which covers repairs, parts, and labor on the engine, auto-

Federal Auto Auction.

This '72 Opel sport coupe sold for $1,701 at an open-air auction of seventy-one surplus federally owned vehicles conducted by the General Services Administration. Unlike virtually all of the other winning bids in the auction, the Opel's sale price was slightly higher than the Blue Book's retail price for the car at the time ($1,625).

In fact, many of the cars at this GSA auction sold for substantially below the low Blue Book (wholesale) value. For instance, a '76 Chevrolet Malibu (eight-cylinder, with automatic transmission, air conditioning, power brakes and power steering) was sold to a bidder for $1,535 although its Blue Book prices were $2,250 (wholesale) and $2,775 (retail). And a '74 Ford Custom sedan (eight-cylinder, automatic transmission, and air conditioning) sold for only $350 though its Blue Book values were then at $900 and $1,275.

The majority of cars at this auction were from five to eight years old, were four-door sedans or wagons, and had been driven more than 50,000 miles. But included in the auction were several pickup trucks, a forty-six passenger bus and one jeep. All had been used by an agency of the federal government previously.

GSA permitted prospective buyers to inspect the cars during the week before the auction. During that time, it was possible to bring a professional mechanic to the lot for an expert evaluation of the vehicle.

GSA mails notices of its auctions to persons who are on its mailing list. You can get on GSA's mailing list by calling your local GSA office or by writing:

General Services Administration
Centralized Mailing List Services
Bldg. 41, Denver Federal Center
Denver, Colorado 80225.

The Department of Defense also conducts automobile auctions of its vehicles. To have your name placed on its mailing list, write:

DoD Surplus Sales
P.O. Box 1370
Battle Creek, Michigan 49016.

In addition, many states and municipalities conduct public auctions of their used motor vehicles, as do some large corporations and utilities.

matic transmission, drive shaft, and differential. You should understand that this means these companies only cover major problems that can develop within the first year you own the car; they don't offer the sort of factory warranty that covers most any problem – major or minor – on new cars.

The rental agencies provide these warranties at least in part to overcome consumer reluctance to purchase cars that have been driven by dozens of drivers (some of whom may be inexperienced and careless) many more miles than normal during their first years. The rental companies claim that their vehicles have been extremely well-maintained, and they often provide detailed service records.

Don't be overawed by the pseudo-scientific charts and analyses of these rental used car sales companies. You should treat any car you're interested in purchasing from them just like you would a car from a private party or another used car dealer. Get it inspected by your own mechanic. Even the biggest rental agency has been known to have misled its customers about the history of cars that had been involved in accidents.

To find out the location of the nearest used car lot in your area for the four largest rental used car agencies, call their toll-free numbers:

Avis	800-331-1212
Budget	800-228-9650
Hertz	800-654-3131
National	800-328-4567

Public Auctions

Unless you're mechanically inclined or are willing to put a lot of money into a car, you probably should steer clear of the public automobile auctions held from time to time by governmental agencies and some large corporations. But devoted clunker mongers can occasionally find real gems for a fraction of the price they'd have to pay elsewhere.

Since most auto auctions are poorly advertised, you'll probably have to make a few phone calls to learn about them. The most common are local police auctions of unclaimed, abandoned vehicles. You can usually find out where and when these auctions are held by calling the local police department. I went to a local police auction a few months ago at which my friend Bill purchased a three-quarter-ton '67 Ford pickup truck for a mere $205. With only a day's labor and about $100 in spare parts, Bill got the truck running in good shape, and it's been working well ever since.

Bill's mechanical ability paid off in this instance since the rules of the auction permitted only a half-hour's inspection of all of the vehicles up for sale that day. Since the city didn't permit the cars to be started in advance it was quite possible that many of the cars wouldn't even run. Not surprisingly, only five of the fifty-five cars up for sale that day were bought.

8 Spotting LEMONS

You've probably heard the old saying "When you buy a used car, you're just inheriting someone else's headaches." Or the adage that, "People only get rid of used cars when they have problems with them."

Both assertions undoubtedly contain more than a kernel of truth. Thousands of persons complain every year that they were burnt by unanticipated, expensive auto repair bills for their recently purchased used cars.

No one knows exactly how frequently this occurs. The Federal Trade Commission looked into the question in the course of its recent extensive investigation into the used car trade. The FTC had a private research company (National Analysts of Philadelphia) conduct a survey in 1977 of 400 used car buyers, who were picked at random from car registration records from twenty different states. According to the National Analysts survey, more than one-third of these buyers (136 of 400) stated that they experienced mechanical problems with their newly bought used cars. The repair bills for these problems ranged from only a few dollars to $1,500 – with the average cost about $110. That is worth repeating: According to this survey, you have a one-in-three chance of experiencing a mechanical problem that will cost an average of $110 to repair soon after buying a used car. You could, of course, be as unlucky as the 18 percent of those with mechanical problems who had to spend more than $201 to get their used cars fixed. In any event, the FTC study underscores why it is important to avoid buying a used car without checking it out carefully.

Remarkably, though, many people take more care in selecting melons in a supermarket than in picking a used car. Gary Ingmire, a used car salesman for the last twenty-six years, tells me that he has had about fifteen customers buy a used car from him without even starting the engine. He says such deals are called "lay downs" in the trade, and he claims they would have happened more often on his used car lot except for his policy of insisting that his customers take a test drive before buying a car.

Ingmire's experience is not unique. According to the previously mentioned survey, 6 percent of the 400 used car buyers stated that they bought their cars without having either "started the car engine on the lot" or even "looked over the car on the dealer's lot."

Why are so many people willing to buy a used car without making the most minimal tests? Ingmire contends it is simply "because they believe the car salesman." But he adds, "Ninety percent of the car salesmen know absolutely nothing about car mechanics. If you gave all the salesmen on an auto row a quiz with twenty easy questions about simple and common mechanical problems with cars, I'll bet you $100 every one of them would flunk the test."

In short, you should never trust the mechanical evaluation of a car by a used car salesman — or by a private party seller, for that matter. That's why you should pay close attention to the advice in this chapter about how to evaluate a used car's mechanical condition.

To start with, you should observe the following cardinal rule in used car buying: NEVER BUY A USED CAR IF THE SELLER REFUSES TO PERMIT AN INDEPENDENT EVALUATION OF THE CAR BY A MECHANIC OF YOUR CHOOSING.

Whether or not you actually plan to have a mechanic look at the car, you should ask the seller if he or she opposes such an inspection. If the seller objects, terminate the process and walk away immediately. It does not matter what the seller's excuse is for not allowing a mechanic's inspection of the car. You have no other way of assuring that the car has no major defects. Most used car salesmen do accept requests for inspections by mechanics. In the FTC survey cited earlier, the dealers agreed to buyers' requests to bring a mechanic to the car lot to do an inspection in 88 percent of the cases, and these same dealers also agreed to buyers' requests to take the car to a mechanic's shop in 92 percent of the instances.

However, most used car buyers simply do not ask to have their cars looked at by mechanics. In the FTC survey, only 27 percent of the buyers surveyed took the cars to "a mechanic or knowledgeable person," while only 14 percent took such a person to the dealer's lot for an inspection. The survey did not differentiate between a mechanic and a knowledgeable person, but the overwhelming percentage of these inspections are conducted by friends of the buyer who are familiar with cars rather than certified mechanics, according to every used car salesman I have interviewed.

TESTS FOR THE MECHANICAL KLUTZ

You don't have to be a mechanic to make some initial tests on a car's mechanical condition. In fact, you can be an outright klutz when it comes to anything more complicated than repairing a fork or spoon but still be able to make a preliminary appraisal on a car.

I've outlined thirteen simple tests that virtually anybody can perform on a used car they are considering purchasing. Included in some of the tests are a few extra steps which someone who is more mechanically inclined (someone I call an MMI) can do. After the first thirteen tests are several others, added especially for the MMIs. Then I've included a few tests that a mechanic should do.

Don't be overwhelmed by these thirteen tests. They are all just a matter of common sense. They are really just a checklist of items you'd probably look for yourself if you decided to look over and then test drive a used car.

I advise you to read over the thirteen tests quickly before you look at a car. Skip the MMI sections in parentheses if you don't plan to conduct those tests yourself. If you feel it would be useful, take the list with you and make notes as you are testing the car. I've left some space for you to do that.

Sure, you may feel like a fool carrying a book with you to a used car lot or to a private seller's house. But you've won half the game once you learn to assert yourself and feel confident about buying a used car your own way. If you let the seller intimidate you out of conducting a few simple tests using this short guide, you'll probably let him intimidate you out of making needed repairs or reducing the price of the vehicle.

Before beginning any test, here are some reminders about testing cars:

1 Most used car salesmen (or private car owners) aren't professional mechanics. Their judgment is suspect for that reason alone, as well as their obvious self-interest in understating mechanical problems. What's more, you should be wary of buying a car from a mechanic. As my mechanic friend Ray Segale says, "Who can disguise a mechanical problem better than a mechanic?"

2 Don't bother testing a car you're not really interested in. You're wasting your time and that of the seller.

Paulette Long and her "Lemon."

Paulette Long resolved to sell her '67 Valiant because it was beginning to rust so badly that she was embarrassed to drive it. She had about one thousand dollars to spend for another car, which she determined would be a subcompact station wagon, such as a Chevrolet Vega, Ford Pinto, Toyota Corona, or Datsun 710.

After a few weeks of scanning newspaper ads, she spied what sounded like an excellent deal: a '75 Pinto wagon for $800 from a private individual. The price sounded great – about $200 to $500 below the typical rate for such cars. The Pinto's owner was a young housewife who told Paulette on the phone that she had mostly driven the car around town for errands. When Paulette drove out to see the car, the owner's husband told her the family had another car that it used for long-distance trips.

Paulette was prepared to buy the Pinto almost as soon as she saw it because its body was in good condition, unlike her ratty-looking Valiant. She brought a mechanically inclined friend along to help her examine the car. The Pinto started immediately for their test drive, and it accelerated well up a hill. Her friend heard no mysterious banging or clanking sounds in the engine, but he did not perform a compression test. Pleased with the car, Paulette paid the $800 in cash. She figured she could not go wrong at that price even if the Pinto possessed a few defects neither she nor her friend had noticed.

A few days after she bought the car, Paulette heard a loud scraping noise when she braked sharply. So she took the car to her friend Jerry, an ex-mechanic. When he took the wheels apart, he discovered that all the brake drums had been scored and needed to be ground. Fortunately, Jerry agreed to volunteer his labor, so the repair only cost her about $30 for the grinding and parts.

A week later, the engine started making a loud knocking noise. A tune-up did not affect the noise, and Paulette had to shell out $280 to have the engine head valves ground. The repair worked in terms of eliminating the noise, but Paulette noticed a few weeks later that a lot of smoke was coming out of the exhaust. When she took the car to a mechanic, he explained that there was a crack in the engine block, which not only caused the smoking but also water to get into the oil and had wrecked the radiator. Because of the free labor of her friend Jerry, Paulette only had to pay $300 for the engine repair and $100 for the radiator, several hundred dollars less than if she had to get the car repaired at any commercial garage.

Paulette had owned her Pinto less than a month, yet she had already spent $710 on repairs – nearly as much as she had spent to purchase the car. What's more, the only reason the repair costs were less than a thousand dollars was the largesse of her ex-mechanic friend, who had worked many hours without compensation.

Paulette did not have to wait long before her Pinto had cost her more than a thousand dollars in repair bills. Less than a month after its smoking engine had been fixed, the Pinto broke down again. This time Paulette was driving up a hill hear her house when the car stopped moving altogether. After getting the car towed to a garage, Paulette learned that the main shaft of the Pinto's automatic transmission had broken, and it cost her $300 to put in a new one.

Paulette vows to have a professional mechanic conduct a thorough inspection of her next used car *before* she buys it.

3 One objective in testing cars before buying them is to weed out potential lemons. Any *major* problem with rust, the brakes, engine, or transmission should eliminate almost any car.

4 Equally important, you are testing a car as part of your bargaining strategy. You want to take careful notes of what you notice as problems with the car, and you want a mechanic to give repair estimates of problems you or he has discovered with the car. In many cases, this list of repair estimates is

your best bargaining tool. If the seller won't reduce the price to accommodate the repairs, he'll frequently make some of the repairs himself to sell the car.

5 Another tactical point. It's often a good idea to ask the seller what he thinks is wrong with the car *before* you begin inspecting it yourself. If the seller had originally been asking $1,500 for the car, you can point out later that he was asking for $1,500 without knowing of the $275 in needed repairs (if he does not mention them). That puts most sellers in a difficult position to defend their initial price.

So, with those points in mind, here are the things you will want to inspect:

Initial, On-the-Lot Tests

Appearance and Comfort: Walk around the car. Are there any obvious flaws that you think would make the car difficult for you to sell later if you bought it? Does it have many dents or scratches? Do any of them look like accident damage? Does it look like it's been repainted (another possible sign of an accident)? Is the front windshield cracked or broken? Are any of the other windows cracked? Do all the doors open properly?

Sit down in the driver's seat. Can you reach all the controls easily – the brake, clutch, gear shift, parking brake, lights, wipers? Can you read the instrument panel clearly?

Try adjusting the driver's seat. If there are bucket seats in front, adjust the other one, too.

Do you have any other initial impressions about the car? Remember to write them down now as you may forget them later.

Lights and Gauges Tests: Ask the seller for the key so you can test all the lights and gauges.

Turn the ignition switch to the "on" position, but do *not* start the car. *If the oil and battery/charge gauges don't come on, stop right there*. It might just be a burnt-out bulb. But then again, it could be something much more serious. Make sure that it's corrected before continuing your inspection. Tell the owner you'll come back once it's fixed.

With the key in the "on" position, you can check out the interior lights and accessories. Here's a checklist:

____ Oil-pressure gauge
____ Battery/charge gauge
____ Temperature gauge
____ Fuel gauge
____ Turn signal blinkers
____ High beam indicator
____ Emergency/warning blinkers
____ Instrument panel lights
____ Horn
____ Windshield wipers and washer
____ Radio
____ Heater fan
____ Cigarette lighter
____ Air conditioner
____ Interior compartment light (when opening door)

Next, you should check how the exterior lights work. You can do it yourself (except for the brake lights) by turning the light switch and then walking to the front or rear of the car. Or you can have someone else turn the light switches while you stand in front of or behind the car. Conduct these tests with the ignition key in the "on" position.

From the front of the car:

________ Parking lights
________ Low beam lights
________ High beam lights
________ Right and left turn signals
________ Emergency/warning flashers

From behind the car:

________ Parking lights
________ Taillights
________ Right and left turn signals
________ Emergency/warning flashers
________ Brake lights
________ Reverse lights
________ License plate lights

On many newer models, you should also check whether the front and rear side lights are working.

Tires: Check the tread depth on all four tires. (MMI: If you put a penny into the tread with Lincoln's head pointed down, tread should reach the top of his head. If not, you'll need to replace those tires soon).

Is the tread worn evenly? (MMI: If it is worn more on one side than the other, it may mean the front end is misaligned – or possibly something more serious, like defective brakes or shocks. If it is worn more on the outside edges than in the middle, it could mean the tire is under-inflated – an indication of poor maintenance.)

Open the trunk and look at the spare tire. If it is worn unevenly, the owner may have recently replaced it with another one to hide a problem. Is there a jack for the car?

(Note: A common trick is to repaint the tires to hide tire wear.)

Rust Tests: My mechanic friend Ray always observes one cardinal rule when buying a used car: NEVER BUY A RUST BUCKET! You can't fix rust. It only gets worse, and severe rust often makes other car repairs more difficult and expensive. Finally, rusted-out bodies can be dangerous, sometimes permitting gas fumes to seep into the passenger compartment.

Walk around the car and look for rusted-out areas. (MMI: Look especially at the rocker panels and under the fenders. If you see any bubbles on the surface of the car, poke at them to see if they cover rusted-out spots. Take a quick look under any mats inside the car. Slam your foot down once on the car floor.)

Leaks: Are there any pools of liquid underneath the car? (MMI: Try to determine if any oil leaks are from the engine, the transmission, or the rear-end differential. Is the radiator leaking water? If you can't tell because the car is sitting over a very dirty spot, wait until you've test driven it and park in a relatively clean spot before looking for leaks.)

Under the Hood: Does the engine look clean or is it very oil-splattered? Does the battery look corroded? (*Note*: A common trick is to steam clean the engine and repaint the hoses and wires.)

(MMI: Check all the fluids. Engine oil dipstick level ______ Any sign of water in the oil? ______ Color of oil ______ Radiator water level ______ Any sign of oil in the water? ______ Brake fluid level ______ Battery fluid level ______ Corrosion at battery terminals or signs of cracked battery? ______ If hydraulic clutch, check fluid level ______ If power steering, check ______ Are the hoses in good shape or do some look cracked? ______ Do the electrical wire terminals look corroded? ______ If an automatic transmission, check the trans oil level after the engine has been warmed up, such as after the test drive ______ Is the trans oil clean and reddish? ______ If it is dark brown or smells burnt, reject the car.)

Brake System: Before you start the car, push down hard on the brake pedal for at least thirty seconds. The pedal should stop well above the floor and stay there without sinking gradually.

Test Driving

Now you're ready to start the engine and take the car for a test drive. Again, let your own common sense tell you whether the car is something you want to invest in.

Cold Starting: Ideally, you should start the engine when it is cold. A warm engine can disguise starting problems.

Does it start quickly after one or, at most, two turns of the key? Listen to the engine. Does it sound normal to you? Or is there knocking, clanking, choking, or other weird sounds?

(MMI: After the car has warmed up briefly, push down hard on the accelerator and look out the rear window. Is there any noticeable smoke coming out the exhaust? If it is white, that may simply mean some water has condensed in the exhaust system. If black, that may just mean the carburetor needs adjustment, or possibly there is a problem with the choke. If blue, the engine is in bad shape – maybe it needs new piston rings. If so reject the car unless the seller is going to knock off the cost of a rebuilt engine from his price. We'll repeat this test during the test drive, but make notes at this point of any smoke you notice.)

Transmission Tests: Now you want to see how well the car shifts into various gears. If you have a few feet of space in which to move the car at the lot, move it back and forth a few times. Is it a hassle to shift? Does it seem to move easily from one gear to the other?

Once you've pulled the car out onto the road, ask for a little silence so you can listen to the car. If the car has an automatic transmission, does it shift smoothly from one gear to the next without any jerking? Do you hear any loud, unusual, or grinding noises as it moves from the low gear to high gear? Make similar notes of any unusual noises from a manual transmission (stick shift), and in addition note whether you have any problems shifting from gear to gear. Do you have to exert any unusual effort to put it into gear?

Steering and Handling: Make a series of left and right turns. Pick a relatively deserted road and turn the wheel back and forth as you drive a zigzag pattern. But be careful not to overdo it until you're certain the car won't go out of control. Take the car to a vacant parking space and parallel park the car. Have you noticed any abnormal problems in handling the car to this point? Any lack of responsiveness to your steering? Is it too tight? Do you like the way it handles?

Brakes: By this time you should know whether the brakes work decently. Now you need to find out how they work under a little stress.

First, find a relatively vacant stretch of road. At about 25 mph, push down on the brakes gently and gradually move your hands off the wheel. Not too far in case the car begins to veer sharply! Do the brakes seem to grab or pull in one direction rather than another? Does the car steer itself toward the right or left?

Now you can test how the brakes work at higher speeds. This time, make sure no one is following closely from the rear. Get the car to go up to about 45 to 50 mph, then hit the brakes hard, holding onto the steering wheel. Do the brakes halt the car quickly and smoothly? Would you feel safe driving the car with the brakes in their present condition?

Engine Performance: While driving the car, you should be listening to the engine. You don't have to be a mechanic to hear unusual sounds like knocking, clanking, howling, screeching. Perhaps only a mechanic can tell you what these noises mean, but you can notice, for instance, if you hear strange engine noises once the car hits about 50 mph. Make notes of anything else you discover about the engine. Does it pick up speed smoothly at lower speeds? Does it seem to have any power to accelerate? Can it climb hills?

(MMI: Another smoke test. Get the car going to about 50 mph, then take your foot off the accelerator and let it slow down to about 25 mph. Then abruptly hit the accelerator and look out the rear window for smoke (or have someone other than the seller do it for you). If you see blue smoke, the car engine probably needs an expensive ring job. Black smoke may mean a carburetor or other tuning problem.)

Other Test Driving Notes: Did you notice whether all the instruments worked while driving? The speedometer? _____ Odometer (mileage record)? _____ Did the temperature gauge indicate the car overheated? _____

If possible, you should drive the car down an alley with your window open. That way you can hear the engine's noises particularly well, and any holes in the muffler or exhaust pipes should be unmistakable.

Also, if possible, you should drive the car over a patch of particularly rough — such as gravel — road. That will tell you a lot about the front suspension.

A final word to the mechanical klutzes: By this time, you should have a good idea about whether the car runs O.K. and whether you feel comfortable about buying it. But remember, you really should have more extensive tests done by somebody who knows a lot more about cars, preferably a professional mechanic. Only the pros can interpret what the problems you may have uncovered mean. Just as important, only the pros can put a realistic price tag on those repairs.

Whatever you do at this point, don't accept the salesman's word about the car's mechanical condition as the final word. His job is to sell cars, not to fix them.

Additional Tests for the More Mechanically Inclined

1 Front End and Shocks: Take hold of each front wheel by grabbing it near the top. Shake it back and forth vigorously. If there is free play and you hear clunking sounds, something is probably wrong with the ball joints or front

suspension. (Repeat on other front wheel.)

You can test the shock absorbers by standing at one corner of the car and pushing it down and up vigorously until it is bouncing. When you release your grip, the car should bounce only one more time and stop abruptly in the middle. (Repeat on the other three corners.)

Another test for the shocks: Drive the car very slowly forward (less than 5 mph), then slam on the brakes. If the front of the car dips down then levels off without continuing to bounce, the shocks are O.K.

Another way to test the car's alignment is to have someone drive the car away from you slowly while you get down on one knee and watch to see if the tires are lined up with the body of the car. If they seem to be going at different angles, or the body is tilted at an angle to the wheels, you may have a serious alignment problem, or the car's frame may be bent from an accident. Be sure to have a mechanic check out this problem.

2 A Never-Fail Clutch Test: My mechanic friend Ray suggests a simple test for the clutch. At about 20 mph, put the car into top gear by pressing the clutch down. Rev up the engine and let the clutch out quickly. If the engine dies, you have a good clutch. If not, it either needs adjustment or replacement.

Auto Diagnostic Clinic.

Many communities have auto diagnostic centers that specialize in inspecting used cars for prospective car buyers. For fees ranging from $15 to $25, these centers can usually provide the buyer with a list of major and minor defects and an estimate of repair costs. This photo shows the center operated by the California State Automobile Association.

The vast majority of prospective car buyers who take cars to one of these centers find the inspections extremely helpful in their auto purchase decisions. In a survey sponsored by the Federal Trade Commission, 88 percent of those who used CSAA's clinic characterized the inspection as having been "very useful" in making a decision about whether to buy the car, while less than 3 percent described the inspection as "not useful." Even more significant, the same FTC-sponsored survey revealed that nearly 85 percent of the used car dealers agreed to perform repairs on the defects discovered by CSAA's clinic, and more than half of the dealers also agreed to drop their original price of the car after being informed of the defects.

CSAA's Diagnostic Clinic mechanics perform more than one hundred separate tests on the vehicles and give the prospective car buyers a written copy of their report. Included in the diagnosis are the following tests: cooling system pressure, tire tread depth, wheel alignment, cranking voltage, carburetion air/fuel rations, road horse power, exhaust system leaks, brake efficiency, and brake linings. The clinic also examines the car engine's ignition with electronic testing equipment and studies its engine and transmission performance with a cylinder-balance/rpm test similar to a compression test.

3 Oil-Burner Test: After you've let the car idle for a couple of minutes, turn off the engine and walk to the back of the car. Stick your fingers inside the exhaust pipe. If the stuff you wipe out of the pipe is a whitish or grayish color, that's fine. But if your finger gets covered with a black and oily substance, you've got a real oil-burner of a car on your hands. It's either got some serious engine problems, or you're going to have to keep filling it with oil.

4 Exhaust System Exam: Jack up the car and take a careful look at the muffler and the connecting exhaust pipes. If you see any holes, or loose connections, you may have to spend a lot to get it fixed.

5 Compression Test: If you've done simple tune-ups, you can probably do an engine compression test without much difficulty. You'll need two tools: a spark plug wrench and a compression tester (a cheap one sells for about $5).

When you remove the spark plugs, make sure you remember which plug goes into which cylinder. Don't clean them, as the mechanic may want to look at them. But you should notice if they all look normal (a tan or dull grayish in appearance) or if some of them are fouled with oil or carbon or look corroded.

The next step is to insert the compression tester into one cylinder at a time. If you have a remote starter switch (they cost about $3), you can do this yourself. Otherwise, you'll have to have someone else crank the engine. The important thing to notice is whether the cylinders all read within ten or fifteen pounds of each other. If not, there's something wrong. Unless you're an experienced mechanic, you probably can't figure out the cause for the discrepancy on your own. But it's a good sign you'd better look for another car to buy.

TESTS FOR THE MECHANIC

If you're still considering buying a car after you've checked it out or one of your MMI friends has checked it out for you, I'd advise having a mechanic do a check. The $15 to $35 you spend for a pro's advice is well worth it.

Let me emphasize that there's a difference between a friend who knows a lot about cars (an MMI) and someone who makes his living repairing cars. Most MMIs (like myself) may have considerable knowledge about their own car or even a few other models. But they usually don't know enough to distinguish serious problems from minor ones, or to give a realistic estimate of how much it would cost to repair a problem. Besides, a mechanic's check-up will usually pay for itself. You can use his estimate of repair costs to bargain with the seller. And if the mechanic discovers some major problems, count yourself among the lucky to have been saved the aggravation and expense of constant auto repairs.

Many cities have auto diagnostic centers which will have their own procedures for testing used cars. You should make sure that if you go to one of these centers it doesn't offer to make repairs on the car. That will not be the kind of independent assessment you are looking for.

If you are going to have an independent mechanic check the car, you might suggest that he do the four tests listed below. He may want to do others as well.

1 Engine compression, or equivalent.

2 Brake inspection. Ask that he pull off a front and rear brake to inspect the linings and check for leaks in the wheel and master cylinders.

3 Check under the car. While the car is on a lift, ask the mechanic to look at the drive shaft, U-joints, and differential, and to see whether there has been any structural damage to the frame from an accident.

4 Test drive the car to determine the mechanic's assessment of how the engine performs and how the transmission and clutch operate.

You should also show him your list of flaws that you've uncovered. Ask him to give you an estimate of how much it would cost to have the car put into tip-top shape.

At this point, you may wish to write up your own estimated cost-of-repair checklist. It may come in handy when you start bargaining over price.

Repair estimate

$________ Engine (including carburetion and ignition)

________ Transmission/clutch/driveline

________ Brakes

_______ Exhaust system
_______ Tires
_______ Suspension (shocks)/alignment
_______ Battery/charging system
_______ Radiator/cooling system
_______ Lights/electrical accessories
_______ Body/frame
_______ Interior
_______ Other

$_______ Total

THREE FINAL TESTS

Before you buy a car, you should assure yourself that: 1. the car's odometer reflects the car's actual mileage; 2. the car has had the necessary maintenance accomplished if it was involved in a manufacturer's recall campaign; and 3. the car is not stolen.

Although federal and state laws strictly prohibit tampering with odometers, some dealers still resort to this tactic. Three things to notice that might indicate tampering:

1 The odometer mileage is considerably less than what can be expected on a car of its age. Most cars are driven between 10,000 and 15,000 miles a year, so a little arithmetic can tell you if a car has far fewer miles than should be anticipated. Many cars are exceptions to the 10,000-miles-plus-per-year average, but you should be wary of cars with unusually low (or high) mileage. At the very least, you should seek an explanation from the seller.

2 The digits of the odometer do not line up properly with each other. Odometers that have been turned back often have misaligned digits between the ten-mile and one-mile or between the one-mile and one-tenth-mile figures. Also, the one-tenth-mile digit sometimes vibrates when the car is moving on odometers that have been altered.

3 The lubrication stickers on the door panels record a higher mileage than that shown on the odometer.

Millions of cars are recalled each year to correct manufacturing defects. Although most of the recalls involve relatively minor problems, some represent major safety hazards. Despite the publicity given these recalls, nearly a third of all recalled vehicles (representing more than 20 million automobiles) have not been taken back to the dealers to be fixed. To find out whether a specific car model (either domestic or foreign) has been subject to a recall, call the National Highway Safety Administration's recall hotline at 800-424-9393. If the car model was recalled, you should ascertain from the seller whether the car was taken in for corrections.

It may be nearly impossible to recover your money if you buy a stolen car from a private party. So it's worth the effort to make sure the car's serial number matches those on the car title and registration papers. On models manufactured since about 1970, the serial number is located on the dashboard on the driver's side of the car. You can normally see the number by looking through the window while standing outside the car. On most domestic cars built before 1968 or 1969, the serial number is located on the body frame next to the door panel on the driver's side. You can see it when you open the car door. One exception is the pre-1970 Volkswagen Beetles whose serial number is located under the back seat next to the battery.

9 The art of HAGGLING

When you go out and buy yourself a TV set, a pair of shoes, or a box of laundry detergent, you usually pay whatever price is marked on the product.

Not so with cars. If you've never bought a car before, you've probably heard that you're expected to haggle over the price with the seller. But you may feel uncomfortable with the thought of bargaining for a product as if you were in a Middle Eastern bazaar.

Unfortunately, any unease you feel about haggling works to the advantage of the seller. If he's a used car salesman, he's a pro at haggling. He's been through it many times before. In the face of a strange process and a knowledgeable opponent, many people become surprisingly passive and agreeable. But there's no reason to be timid. It's not a mysterious process, and the bottom line is that you might save yourself hundreds of dollars for a few minutes of effort.

Here's my five-step method to learn the art of better haggling:

1 Don't start bargaining until you're seriously interested in a specific car. You'd not only be wasting the seller's time, but you may hurt your credibility when it comes time to do some real haggling.

2 Know the market value of the car. (See the section below on "Demystifying the Blue Book.")

3 After you have had the car inspected (see Chapter 8, "Spotting Lemons"), list all of the car's defects along with estimates of how much they'd cost to repair. Use this list as a bargaining lever to get the price lowered or to try to get the needed repairs accomplished without having the price increased.

4 Arrange your financing in advance. If you have your cash ready, you'll be in a better position to bargain. More important, you'll know exactly what your maximum price is so you don't get sucked into some complicated financing arrangement with the seller.

5 *Be prepared to say no and mean it*. Ultimately, your only power is to reject the deal. If you're not ready to pass up a car for another one, your bargaining position is immensely weakened.

DEMYSTIFYING THE BLUE BOOK

You've probably heard of the "Blue Book" even if you've never bought a used car before. By the time you go through the car-buying process, you will have heard the phrase many times. Even then it's doubtful you'll ever see an actual Blue Book, and you may wonder whether it really exists.

It does. In fact, there are two publications employed by used car dealers that are commonly referred to as "the bible," "the book" the "Blue Book," or the "Red Book."

The *Kelley Blue Book* is published every other month by an independent company based in Costa Mesa, California, while the National Automobile Dealers Association of Washington, D.C. puts out a monthly *NADA Official Used Car Guide*. Both are used throughout the industry, though some areas of the country rely more on one publication than the other (Kelley is more prevalent in the West).

Both Kelley and NADA list the wholesale and retail prices for almost every make and model and style of domestic and import car produced within the last six years. They base their values on their surveys with selected car retailers throughout the country.

Significantly, neither publication is sold to the general public. But virtually every used car salesman in the country gets either Kelley or NADA, and most banks, credit unions, and libraries subscribe to one of them too. Feel free to call up any of these sources to find out the current "book prices" of any model you are interested in. It's an extremely common practice.

At least two other companies — Edmund's and Buyer's Guide Reports — publish their own guides to used car prices for both domestic and foreign cars

"Beautiful" Bob White and the Blue Book

manufactured in the last six or seven years. Both put out revised guides four times a year. Edmund's has been publishing its guides since 1968, while Buyer's Guide Reports has been in business since 1974. Unlike *Kelley* or *NADA*, you can buy these paperback guides directly, either from local newsstands or by mail directly from the publishers. In my experience, each publisher responds immediately to all mail-order requests. Below are the addresses for both publishers:

Edmund's Used Car Prices Single copies, $1.95, plus 50¢ postage and handling; one-year subscription (four copies), $7.50. Order from: Edmund's Subscription Department, UCP-479, 515 Hempstead Tpke., West Hempstead, NY 11552. (Book stores can order Edmund's from Dell Distributors of New York.)

Buyer's Guide Reports Used Car Prices: Single copies, $1.95, plue 50¢ postage and handling; one-year subscription (four copies), $6. Order from DMR Publications, Inc., 1410 E. Capitol Dr., Milwaukee, Wis. 53211.

(Note: Both Edmund's and Buyer's Guide Reports also publish similar paperbacks that list prices for new domestic cars, new foreign cars and new vans, trucks and pickups. Single copies of each are $1.95.)

Neither Edmund's nor Buyer's Guide Reports publishes price figures that are identical to *Kelley's* or *NADA's* (nor do the two "official" publications print the same amounts). Nevertheless, both of the consumer publications publish figures that are comparable to the standard guides, and you may find one of these paperbacks useful if you expect to look at a lot of different cars.

Finally, there is no Blue Book for cars older than six or seven years. As I mentioned in Chapter 4, the price of older cars is often determined as much by the condition of a specific car as by its original retail list price.

That doesn't mean you can't get some idea about the general market value of older cars from other sources. First, you can consult the Blue Book's listing of similar models that are somewhat younger. For instance, if you're interested in a 1969 Chevrolet Nova, you can discover the Blue Book price for the 1973 version of the same model in one of the guides described above. In the summer of 1979, the '73 Nova 6 two-door coupe was listed as retailing for $1,400 and wholesaling for $1,025. You can assume that a '69 Nova ought to sell for at least several hundred dollars less than the retail price of the '73 Nova.

Another method for determinig a reasonable price range for an older car: Look in the newspaper want-ads in your area for similarly aged vehicles. Though want-ad prices are generally somewhat higher than what people actually pay for those automobiles, you can get an idea of what you should expect to pay from the want-ads.

Also, a Texas publisher named Quentin Craft puts out what he calls *The Gold Book*, which lists prices for cars produced between 1946 and 1970. Instead of listing the retail and wholesale prices of used cars, *The Gold Book* lists car values based on the condition of the cars — "fair, good, or excellent."

You can get a copy of this guide by sending $7.95 to The Gold Book, 910 Tony Lama St., El Paso, Texas 79915.

Using the Blue Book to Your Advantage

All of the publications listed above — *Kelley*, *NADA*, Edmund's, Buyer's Guide Reports — purport to list the "average" retail and wholesale prices of used cars. To bargain most effectively with a car seller, you have to know the significance of these figures.

Let's look at a specific example in order to examine this issue further. According to a recent edition of the *Kelley Blue Book*, the "average wholesale" price of a '72 Mercury Marquis (two-door hardtop with a V-8 engine) was $1,025, while its "average retail" price was $1,630.

In other words, the difference between those two figures, or $605, is what the typical middleman — such as a used car dealer — is currently profiting from selling that particular model of car. That's right. According to its surveys of the used car market, the "average" used car retailer is out there buying '72 Mercury Marquises for $1,025, spending a few bucks to "recondition" the car, and selling the same car for $605 more than he paid for it! Sounds like a good racket, eh?

How can you use this information for your own benefit? Say that you're interested in buying a '72 Mercury Marquis from a private party. Once you've found out the actual "book" wholesale value of the car, you know how much the car's owner can expect to get if he were to sell it to a car dealer. You can generally assume that the only reason he's interested in selling it himself is that he thinks he can get more for it from you than he could from a dealer. He may have already tried to sell it to a dealer and found out the hard way that all he's going to get is $1,025, and possibly less if there's anything the dealer finds wrong with the car. Most dealers use the book wholesale price as the starting point and make deductions for flaws from there.

As your first move, you should offer no more than the book wholesale price, minus your estimate of what repairs are essential. In other words, *you should feel comfortable about offering a private party exactly what a dealer would offer, regardless of how much the owner is asking for the car*. After all, the owner isn't going to get any more by selling it to a car lot. Anything more that you offer is just gravy for him.

Let's say that the owner was originally asking $1,800 for the car and that he rejects your offer of $1,000 out of hand. If he's offended by your offer, you can explain to him that you are merely offering the book value of the car, minus $25 because you noticed that the car needs upholstery covers for both seats. If $1,000 is too little, you might ask, what was he thinking about?

Nine times out of ten, you can expect a private party to knock off a lot of money at this point in the bargaining. You have shown that you know what you're talking about. If you're sincerely interested in buying the car, you ought to expect some flexibility on his part. What's more, many private car owners tend to overestimate the value of their own cars. It might come as a complete shock to him that $1,025 is all he can expect to get for his car from a dealer. You might suggest that he call up any dealer and ask what they'd offer – you have nothing to lose.

In the best possible circumstances, you might succeed in getting the private owner to use your initial offer as the basis for subsequent bargaining. If possible, you should make him try to convince you that the car is worth more than the book wholesale price. You're in a much better position when he's on the defensive than if you are trying to defend your offer.

Of course, there are many other possibilities that can enter into play. The owner may say he has received higher offers. These may be serious offers, or the owner may be bluffing. In either case, you are in a stronger position if you are prepared to pay on the spot. The proverbial bird in the hand is always a powerful argument.

Whatever you do, *avoid bidding any higher than the book's retail price*. Just as the owner wouldn't bother trying to sell the car unless he thought he could get more than he could from a dealer, you certainly shouldn't buy the car at a price you could probably get from a dealer.

(One subtle point: If the owner isn't aware of the book's retail price for the car, you won't help your case by telling him. It's better to stick with the wholesale price.)

Finally, *never bid higher than the maximum you planned to spend originally*. You'll only regret it later. Stick to your final offer. Be prepared to walk away. Leave your name and number with the owner and tell him that if he changes his mind, he should give you a call.

I had a friend named Charlie who bought a '74 Plymouth Duster privately. He and the former owner could not agree on a price. The owner wanted $2,000, but Charlie was only willing to pay $1,500 (which was about $100 above the book wholesale price). Charlie really wanted the car, but he just didn't want to borrow more money to get it. Three days later Charlie got a call from the owner asking if he'd still be willing to buy the car for $1,500. The owner hadn't been able to find anyone else who'd buy it for $2,000.

HAGGLING WITH A PRO

Bargaining with a used car salesman is similar. But you can assume from the outset that he will make at least a modest profit from the deal and that he can out-bargain you with his eyes closed. He is a pro; you're not. But don't let his experience intimidate you. Remember that he depends on people like you to make his living. He needs your business more than you need a particular car.

Again, you should be familiar with "the book" prices of any car you're seriously interested in buying. If a dealer selling that same '72 Mercury Marquis is asking for more than the book's retail price, you should point that out to the salesman and make him justify the higher price tag. You're always best off if you try to make the seller defend his price.

Before going any further in this discussion about bargaining with a used car salesman, you should be aware of the difference between the salesman working in a car dealership and the dealer himself, referred to by many salesmen as "the house." For one thing, the salesmen often don't know 1) who the previous owner of the car was or how the car was acquired, 2) how much "the house" paid for the car, or 3) what the minimum amount "the house" will accept for the car. Consequently, you may discover that when you start to bargain with a used-car salesman, he will begin to act as if he were merely a middleman between you and the owner of the business. You may think that this is merely a salesman's ploy, but frequently it is the absolute truth. (See the next chapter for more insight into the games these men play, especially about "Playhouse 90.")

At the same time, don't think that any used car salesman is your buddy. He may know exactly how much the dealer paid for the car, and so forth. Worse, he may be aware of mechanical defects in the car but never volunteer that information to you.

Unfortunately, it appears that many used car salesmen knowingly mislead customers about cars' mechanical problems. In a survey commissioned by the Federal Trade Commission, the California Public Interest Research Group had a team of researchers pose as prospective used car purchasers at a number of used car lots in the San Diego area during January 1977. One researcher would express interest in a car and then ask to have it taken to a auto diagnostic center for a complete mechanical inspection. That researcher would bring back the car and inform the salesman of the results of the inspection, including the estimated cost of repairs of the defects disclosed by the mechanical examination. Subsequently, CALPIRG sent a second researcher who asked to see the same vehicle. The result: In 75 percent of the cases, the "used motor vehicle salespeople did not inform prospective purchasers of mechanical defects which the salespeople knew to exist," according to CALPIRG.

Some of the salesmen in this survey engaged in blatant lying. One car selling for $1,299 was found to have serious engine problems (a possible cracked head or cracked block), loose steering, maladjusted valves and a number of other minor defects. CALPIRG's "revisitor" asked the same salesman who had been given the original copy of the diagnosis by the initial surveyor if the salesman knew of any mechanical defect in the car. The salesman replied, "It was checked out the other day, and it came out real good . . . only minor crap" was wrong with it.

In another instance, a salesman accompanied the initial test buyer to the diagnostic center where it was discovered that the car needed a complete brake job, had one bald tire, both the left and right front side lights were inoperative, its fuel line was leaking and needed replacement, along with a plethora of other minor defects. Nevertheless, the salesman told CALPIRG's revisitor that the only faults revealed in the diagnosis were a bad muffler and a cracked dashboard. What's more, the salesman had upped the price of the car two hundred dollars!

In the face of such practices, it is clear that any wise used car buyer needs all the ammunition he or she can muster when haggling with a professional used car salesman. Besides an awareness of the Blue Book prices, an independent mechanical examination of the car (preferably by a mechanic) is undoubtedly the best tactic available. As you can see from Table 9.1, car buyers who used the results of the mechanic's diagnoses as part of their bargaining strategy succeeded more often than not. They usually either got the price of the car reduced, or they got the dealers to perform the needed repairs at no additional cost.

Above all else: Remember that you are in a business relationship with any used car salesman. His primary objective is to make a profit from the transaction; yours is to pay as little as possible. Almost every used car salesman knows that he is selling himself as much, or even more, than selling a car. Appearing to be a nice, friendly fellow is the most important tool of his trade. You should consider a used car salesman's smile to be as genuine as a politician's. It's part of the job.

Whatever you do, try not to succumb to the pressure that a professional used car salesman will inevitably put on you. The key word in his vocabulary is "now." He'll want to know whether you are prepared to put down a deposit "now," whether you are ready to make a deal "now," whether you want the car he is showing you "now" if he cuts its price a few hundred bucks, and so forth. He knows that once you leave his car lot you may be gone for good, never to return. He has one chance to get you to commit yourself, and that is now. Frequently, a used car salesman will try to convince you that a car you are considering will be sold to someone else if you don't make a commitment immediately. Sometimes that happens. But it is more important for you to take that risk than buy a car at a higher price than you are prepared to pay.

Remember that the most important word in bargaining with a used car salesman is PATIENCE. The more anxious you appear, the less willing a pro will be to lower the price of the car. As well, time is on your side. *The more time you can devote to buying a car, the more money you are likely to save in the long run, and the better the car you are likely to buy for the money you spend.* It's easy to forget that almost self-evident fact when a professional salesman is going through his routine.

GUARANTEES AND WARRANTIES

Before completing a deal for a used car, the salesman may offer to give you a guarantee or warranty on the car. If he does not, you should try to obtain one, if possible. Before considering the wide variety of guarantees, keep in mind the following principles:

1. Verbal assurances of any kind do not constitute a legal guarantee. If a used car dealer is unwilling to translate his oral promises to writing before you purchase a vehicle, you can imagine how difficult it will be to get him to agree to make repairs if something goes wrong with the car. You should also be aware that if you ever try to take a dealer to court on the basis of his verbal agreements alone, you will have almost no chance of getting a sympathetic hearing from a judge.

2. In most states, a dealer is required to certify certain safety devices or features of the car — such as the brakes, the lights and turn signals, and the

smog control equipment – without any extra guarantee. You can find out what the dealer must certify by calling up your local office of your state's Department of Motor Vehicles, or equivalent.

3 Your best guarantee is a careful mechanical inspection of a car in advance of purchase. Trying to obtain repairs from a dealer is almost always a major hassle and headache even with the most airtight written guarantee from the most honorable and responsible used car dealer. An ounce of prevention. . . .

4 The time limits on a guarantee are absolute. If a dealer writes that he will guarantee all or part of a vehicle for thirty days, he does not mean thirty-one.

"As Is"

The most common used car guarantee is called "as is," which is actually no guarantee at all. It means that you are buying the car in its current condition and that the seller assumes no further responsibility for the vehicle. Period.

Parts/Labor Guarantee

Another common guarantee states that in case something goes wrong with the car within the time period of the guarantee or warranty, the dealer will assume responsibility for the parts involved in the repair and the purchaser will have to pay for the labor. Or, in other cases, such guarantees are written the opposite way, with the purchaser having to buy the parts and the dealer agreeing to take care of the labor costs.

This may sound attractive, but in many instances, used car dealers have been known to artificially inflate the buyer's half of the agreement to cover his costs. For instance, let's say that two weeks after you bought a car with a thirty day parts/labor guarantee, the car's muffler develops a hole causing a loud noise when you drive the car. According to the terms of your warranty, the dealer said he would take care of the parts while you would pay for the labor. So you take your car back to him for repairs, and he has his mechanic perform the repairs. When you get your car back, you get a bill for fifty dollars, which includes two hours' labor at twenty-five dollars an hour. What probably happened is that the repair only took one hour (or less) and the dealer merely added on another hour of labor costs to cover what he had to spend to buy a new muffler. (In fact, it may have been cheaper for you to have gone to another repair shop that specializes in mufflers than to have had it taken care of by the used car dealer.)

Fifty-Fifty Split

A variation of the parts-labor guarantee is one that states that in case a repair must be performed within the time period, the dealer agrees to split the cost in half with the buyer. This type of agreement has the same pitfall as the parts-labor guarantee. In many cases, the dealer will simply inflate the repair bill to the point that you wind up paying for the actual costs of the repair.

Drive-Train Warranty

Some guarantees are written to cover only one part of the vehicle, often just the drive train, also known as the power train. Usually this means the engine, clutch (if there is one), transmission, and possibly the differential. In other words, this kind of warranty takes care of the most expensive common repair, though these parts of the car are also less likely to break down.

One problem with this type of warranty: Often, a drive-train warranty is written in such a way as to absolve the dealer of any responsibility in case the driver has abused or in any way caused the mechanical failure. I know of a case where a fellow named Jimmy bought a late-model used car with a ninety day drive-train warranty. Several weeks after he bought the car, the engine blew up, and Jimmy had the car towed to the dealer. When Jimmy returned to pick up his car, the dealer informed him that his mechanic discovered that the oil was low in the engine and that it was his opinion that the engine blew up because Jimmy had not properly maintained the vehicle. To fix the car's engine would cost a thousand dollars, the dealer said.

Warranty Insurance

Some dealers offer a full guarantee for parts and labor for a certain fee, often through a separate warranty insurance company. A typical charge might be one to three hundred dollars in exchange for one- or two-years' coverage.

As with any kind of insurance policy, repair insurance is a gamble. It is always more likely that you will spend more on the insurance than the insurance company will pay you for the car repairs during the period covered by the warranty. Otherwise the company would not offer you the policy. On the other hand, if your car's engine blows up or the transmission freezes, this kind of insurance would save you a lot of money.

Two things to remember before buying this kind of warranty. First, most of these policies have deductible clauses, similar to the deductible provisions of auto insurance, collision or comprehensive coverage. If the deductible is one hundred dollars, that means you will have to pay for the first one hundred

Car Salesman Robert Roebling

dollars of any repair. That means you are only covered for a major repair job since most common auto repairs are less than one hundred dollars. And you have to pay at least one hundred dollars of a major repair.

Second, make sure to read the small print of this kind of warranty (as you should *any* auto guarantee or warranty). In most cases, the insurer has no responsibility if you are shown to have caused the mechanical problem through abuse or neglect. Just as with Jimmy and his blown engine, you may not have the kind of total coverage you assumed you had when you purchased the car.

Full Guarantee

The ideal guarantee provides for 100 percent coverage for any mechanical defect that appears within a certain time period. Some even offer the buyer a replacement car in case the original car cannot be repaired easily. This is, of course, the best kind of guarantee, and many reputable used car dealers give full guarantees because they are interested in repeat business.

Table 9.1 Results of AAA Diagnostic Tests on Used Cars

	CSAA[1]	ACMo.[2]
Defects *not* reported to prospective buyer before diagnosis	92.6%	95.8%
Average repair estimate for defects discovered by tests	$162.89	$235.64
Buyers who asked dealers to perform needed mechanical work	69.4%	69.4%
Dealers who agreed to perform needed mechanical work	84.7%	84.7%
Dealers who agreed to reduce price of car because of needed mechanical work	55.6%	33.8%
Buyers no longer interested in car because of defects	11.9%	21.0%
Buyers who agreed to buy the car that was inspected	80.6%	68.0%

1. The California State Automobile Association conducted auto diagnostic tests on 300 prepurchase vehicles between January 1976 and January 1977 for this study that was commissioned by the Federal Trade Commission. The vehicles were selected at random from cars that underwent prepurchase inspections at CSAA's diagnostic clinics in either San Francisco or San Jose.

2. The Automobile Club of Missouri conducted a similar survey for the FTC of vehicles inspected at the club's diagnostic clinics at St. Louis and Kansas City.

What to Do if Burnt

As I have tried to stress earlier in this chapter and in Chapter 8, "Spotting Lemons," your best protection from buying a lemon occurs *before* the purchase. You usually have little recourse after the fact, especially without an ironclad written guarantee that a dealer absolutely refuses to honor. If you buy a car from a private party, you have even less legal ground to stand on in most cases.

If, despite all your precautions, you find yourself stuck with a mechanical nightmare, you should do the following:

1. Try to work out the problem with the seller. Many times you will be able to arrange for certain repairs to be made even though they are not covered by your warranty, especially if you can make a convincing case that you were given some kind of verbal assurances in advance. Usually you should try to talk directly with the dealer or sales manager rather than with a salesman. Make sure to keep all the written documents pertaining to the car and to put your complaint in writing to the dealer.
2. Contact the Better Business Bureau and/or the local or state consumer affairs office. Sometimes these agencies can put pressure on dealers.
3. Take the case to small claims court. In many states, small claims court is an ideal place to fight your battle with a car dealer over a repair. Check with the court in your area to find out how to file a claim.
4. Sue the dealer. Your ultimate recourse is to hire a lawyer and take the dealer to court. This can be very expensive and cost more than the car did originally. But if you have a legitimate claim, this may be the only way you have to achieve justice.

10 CONFESSIONS of used car salesmen

Richard Nixon is not the only politician who has been the butt of the standard "Would you buy a used car from . . ." joke. The stereotype of deceitful used car salesmen is so widespread that it is common even in Europe. During one British election several years ago, *Punch*, the British humor magazine, printed a cartoon with a caricature of the Conservative Party's Edward Heath. In the cartoon, the candidate for prime minister is shown standing in a boat, asking, "Would you buy a used boat from this man?"

In her sociological study of used car salesmen, *The Used Car Game: A Sociology of the Bargain* (Heath, 1973), Dr. Joy Browne describes the common public perception of used car salesmen: "Not only are used car salesmen purportedly unethical, unfair and a group against which one has to be constantly on guard, but they are so evil that nothing is too low to try on them, lying, cheating, chicanery, flattery, or if all else fails, a little sex."

Indeed, used car salesmen are often considered to be the last of a vanishing breed of old-fashioned hucksters and flim-flam men. Many people believe they have nothing but tricks up their sleeves. Moreover, they are seen to share a kind of semi-secret bond, wherein only the initiates are granted access to the reality behind their constant sleights of hand.

Aspects of this stereotype have considerable validity. Many people have been ripped off by used car salesmen who either outright lied to them or told partial truths about important questions. What's more, used car salesmen as a group are an identifiable subculture, with its own mores and jargon.

In the past year, I've watched dozens of used car salesmen ply their trade while helping numerous friends and acquaintances buy used cars. Though I developed quite a familiarity with their selling techniques, I still felt like an outsider to their tight world. So I decided to try to interview some of these men (as yet there are extremely few used car saleswomen) to see if they would tell me more details about their business.

I quickly discovered that interviewing used car salesmen for publication was not going to be easy. They tend to be extremely extroverted and gregarious individuals, particularly when meeting the public. But I found most of them surprisingly suspicious and guarded when I suggested doing a candid interview. Most simply refused to talk openly about their business, while others insisted on anonymity. In particular, salesmen who worked for large new or used car dealerships were loathe to cooperate — I sensed that many feared reprisals from their bosses. Others seemed to refuse because they felt they would be violating a kind of unspoken bond not to reveal the trade secrets. Some may have felt that to talk frankly about their business would ultimately jeopardize their livelihood. I couldn't honestly disagree with that perception since it is probably true that the profit margin for the used car middlemen would be cut markedly if the buying public understood more about used cars, such as their actual market values and mechanical condition.

Slowly, I won the trust of several used car salesmen who ultimately consented to interviews. What follows are some of the high points of those conversations.

David Pritikin — An Old Timer

David Pritikin has managed a small used car lot in the Brownsville section of Brooklyn, New York, for less than a year. But his involvement as a professional used car salesman, wholesaler and dealer dates back more than thirty years to the period immediately after the Second World War.

At that time, new cars were just beginning to be built again after a five-year hiatus during the war. Because of the stoppage of new car production during the war, Pritikin recalls, people changed their attitudes about older cars. He says that "Before the war, people would drive their cars 18,000 or 30,000 miles and then get rid of them. But the war proved that cars could go over 100,000 miles." And with the return of thousands of GIs from overseas, the demand was high for these used cars that had kept running during the war years.

Pritikin decided to take advantage of this situation. He bought a '39 LaSalle for $500 and "manicured" the car by cleaning the interior, installing new carpeting, steam cleaning the engine, and generally making the car "look like new." He recalls that many cars of that vintage had a porcelain cover on the engine's exhaust manifold, which he even simonized.

Although gas was relatively expensive in 1947 at 28¢ per gallon, Pritikin had no difficulty selling the LaSalle with its gas-guzzling V-8 engine. He placed an ad in the newspaper asking for $975 for the car, and the first man to see the car liked it so much that he paid cash on the spot.

Pritikin was now in the used car business. Operating from his home, he bought and sold more than a half dozen cars in the same manner, but soon the New York State motor vehicle department began to get after him for selling used cars without a dealer's license.

Rather than drop out of the lucrative used car trade (or try to circumvent the law), Pritikin went to look for a job on Coney Island Avenue, a major auto row in Brooklyn with thirty to forty car lots. After landing a job selling cars with one dealer ($25 per car), he eventually joined with two other salesmen to form a used car partnership called Circle Motors, which operated a fifty-five-car lot on Coney Island Avenue from 1950 to 1973 (when Burger King bought the property).

Pritikin agreed to serve as his firm's principal buyer. So almost every working day for twenty-three years he went to a four-block stretch along Jerome Avenue in the Bronx where about twenty used car wholesalers have lots, each with space for thirty to forty cars. These wholesalers buy cars primarily from new car dealers (who obtain their cars from trade-ins) but also from renting and leasing agencies, and from overstocked used car dealers. The wholesalers do not sell their vehicles to the general public; instead, they confine their trade almost exclusively to used car dealers (like Pritikin), who come to the Bronx from the entire metropolitan area.

These auto wholesalers do not make much profit on each car since their income is based on the tremendous volume of vehicles they turn over. For instance, Pritikin said, it would be common for a car that the wholesaler bought for $4,000 to be sold to a used car dealer for $4,200. A car that was bought for $500 might be sold for $550 or even $525.

Jerome Avenue no longer boasts of its "speedometer men," three or four men who carried their tools in push carts as they moved from lot to lot. In the early years, Pritikin said he paid from $2 to $5 for these men to "clock" a car—that is, flip back the first two digits of the odometer of a high-mileage vehicle. "A car with about 90,000 miles would be flipped back to show only 50,000 miles," Pritikin recalls. "Cars would be flipped three or four times, every time they were sold." By 1973, when the law finally began to crack down on this practice, the "speedometer men" were charging about $10 per car ($15 for Cadillacs because they had to disassemble the dashboards) for jobs that took ten to fifteen minutes to accomplish.

With the federal odometer law in the early 1970s, the FBI caught some of these "speedometer men" and a few wholesalers who falsified mileage registration records, and some went to jail and paid big fines. "Once this law started getting enforced, we stopped doing it," Pritikin admits. "But there's a lot of dealers, unscrupulous dealers, who still do it. They buy these big high mileage cars cheap and they turn them back to forty from ninety thousand miles because you can get a lot more money for that car. There's a lot of Southern dealers who come up to New York from South or North Carolina to buy these big, high-mileage cars, and they clock 'em." But Pritikin insists few New York dealers still do this because "a lot of dealers here have been taught lessons."

Pritikin estimates that during its twenty-three years Circle Motors sold more than 10,000 cars – most of which he bought from Bronx wholesalers. I asked him what he looks for in a used car when he is inspecting it. Pritikin outlined his basic procedures for checking for accident damage, rust, flood damage, and transmission or engine defects.

Accident Damage: "When I buy a car, I look at the chassis to see if it tracks – that the front wheels line up with the rear wheels. You can do that when the car is standing still or by watching it from behind when it moves. Or you can tell when you drive it. If it pulls to one side, it's either chassis damage or very bad alignment.

"You can also look at the tires. If they are all cupped up and scuffed, you know that the car is going sideways, like a rubber eraser. If the front tires are being erased, you have an inkling of chassis damage, which is very expensive to fix. People don't want to drive a car like that.

"I also check to see whether the hood doesn't line up properly or whether there are any wavy lines as you look down the side of the car. And you can tell whether it's been repainted by looking under the rubber gaskets on the doors, or at the fire wall behind the engine where all the gauges and instruments are. They never paint in those spots."

Rust: "Rust is very hard to cover up, and lots of times with today's cars, a lot of rust is coming through after only four or five years. We usually open up the trunk and look down in the fender wells in the corner. If there's water, you know that there's water leaking. You stick your fingers down in the corner, and if you feel water down there, you know you've got a water job."

Flood Damage: "There's a lot of cars I passed up because they were flooders, cars that were hit by a flood or lay in water from a storm. Lots of times you can smell the water inside the car. But you can also rub your fingers under the springs of the seat cushions to see if there's rust. Flooders are very bad. Water gets into the transmission and the brakes, and you have to spend thousand of dollars to replace everything."

Automatic Transmission: "I pull out the transmission stick. The oil is supposed to be red, but if it's brown, the first thing I do is smell it. If it's burnt, it means you will need a transmission job very soon. They cost $400 to replace today."

Engine: "I always check the motor oil to make sure there is no grease in it. Black doesn't mean anything. But if you see a lot of new oil, fresh oil, that means the car could be a smoker, especially if the oil was not changed lately. People keep putting oil in it so the oil would be clean all the time because it goes right out of the exhaust.

"The first thing I do is to start the engine and give it a shot of gas. If you don't see any smoke coming out, it's in good, healthy condition. Then I stick my finger in the tailpipe. If it is dry and not greasy, the engine is in good shape. There should be a dry ash in the back, but if you see a lot of soot and oil in the tailpipe, you know it's burning oil and you will need a motor job.

"Also, the motor has got to be quiet. If you hear a lot of rattling and noise in the engine, you know you've got bad lifters, rocker arms, and push rods. That can run into a few hundred dollars to repair. A little squeak of the fan belt doesn't mean anything."

Power Steering: "Then I check the power steering pump and steering post to see that there's no seal leaks there. I know exactly what everything is going to cost to fix. So I know if the car is worth the money they are asking. Say if it's got a little leak in the power steering, maybe it needs an oil ring. If it needs a little body work, I know how much that body work is going to cost me. I also know what that car will bring retail, so I know whether it pays to buy the car."

Once Pritikin buys a car, he has it "detailed from bumper to bumper." Though Circle Motors had two porters to steam clean the engines, fix the upholstery, wax the car, and so on, it occasionally had to send some cars to other professional detail shops which charged $25 per car (though he says they now charge about $50).

The reason for the detailing is simple. "When it's filthy, people would pass it up. I could get $100 more because it's beautiful."

Maximizing his profits is, after all, the ultimate objective of Pritikin's careful car-buying habits. "In all my years of experience, I've always looked for a clean, straight, low mileage car so that when we sell it we make a friend — with the least amount of money being spent on the car. Most of my business is repeat business because we gave a man a good guarantee — a ninety-day warranty — and stood behind it. We had two mechanics that took care of them immediately, so they recommended other people."

Since Pritikin has always specialized in the bigger, luxury automobiles, the current gas crisis has reduced demand for his cars. At the same time, however, it has had its good side effects. "Right now we can buy big cars very reasonably. For instance, I just bought a '76 Buick Electra Limited — gorgeous with stereo, air conditioning, mag wheels, tilt steering wheel and cruise control, eight-track — a loaded car. It had 5,000 miles on it — 105,000 miles, that is. We bought it cheap. It cost about $12,000 new, but we paid only $1,500 for a '76 Limited.

"Yesterday, a fellow came in and said, 'Gee, that's a nice car. How much you want for it?'

"So I says, 'The car's worth $3,995, but it has a lot of miles on it. So I'll sell it for $2,500.'

"Then he says, 'No. But I like the car. I'll give you $2,000 for it.'

"So I says, 'You just bought yourself a car.' "

Gary Ingmire

"If this car was perfect, I wouldn't have it. The original owner would," Gary Ingmire explains as we stand looking at a green '73 Ford LTD on his used car lot in San Francisco's Latino Mission district. His lot is located across the street from where his father once sold used cars.

Ingmire tells me he picked up the LTD from a new car dealer for $550, and he spent another $30 to have the car "detailed" (polished, thoroughly cleaned and the engine steam cleaned). Painted in white on the LTD's windshield is "$899, RUNS GOOD." Ingmire explains that when the sales tax and license fees are added, the total cost of the car ("the out-the-door price") will be nearly $1,000, or $972.50.

He expects to get every penny of that, too. "I'm hard when I talk prices with people. I expect everyone to haggle. When people say, 'What's your discount?' I say, 'It's already on the window.'

"I keep saying, 'That's what the price is. That's what it is.' If I say 'no' enough, they are going to believe me. If they say, 'I'll give you a hundred bucks less,' I say, 'Get out of here. I don't have to do business with you. That car is cheap.' I stress that they can go to a new car dealer up the street and find the same '73 Ford LTD for $1,800 or $1,900. Their car may be a little cleaner – it may have new tires on it – yet it is the same car.

"Generally, most deals are less than the asking price. But not here. I'll ask the people, 'How much do you think I make on these cars?' Of course, I don't tell them how much I paid for the cars because they wouldn't take my overhead into account." Ingmire says he spends nearly a thousand dollars a month to rent the space for the lot (which holds fifteen to twenty cars), and another $700 a month for insurance. (He has been selling at a rate of nearly one car a day.)

Nevertheless, Ingmire admits he occasionally reduces the asking price for his cars. "If some fellow wanted the LTD and reached into his pocket and said, 'All I've got is $900. Take it or leave it,' then I probably would take it."

Don't expect any assistance from Ingmire if something goes wrong with your car later. "All my business is cash and carry. I take your money, you take my car. I don't want to see you again until you come in and buy another car. It's not guaranteed; it's not warranted; it's yours. It says, 'AS IS' in big letters on the contract, and that's how I sell my cars. When I bought the car from the dealer, he didn't guarantee the car."

Ingmire delivers his sales pitches with a kind of boyish freshness, though it is apparent he has probably used variations of the same rap since he started working for his father in the early 1950s when he was in high school. During the summers, his father agreed to pay him for being a "bird dog" – someone who hustles customers for a car dealer. Ingmire liked to go to the Oakland Army Base where he told Korea-bound and returning GIs about how they could get a good used car cheap at his father's car lot. For each customer who bought a car as a result of Ingmire's activities, his father paid him $50.

Gary Ingmire

Ingmire says his father also used taxi drivers, hotel bell boys, and travel agents as "bird dogs" – and paid them $100 per car. "Bird dogging is still very common in the car business," according to Ingmire. "Lots of good car salesmen have people out there trying to hustle up business."

During his car selling career (which includes having worked as a new and used car salesman for eight different new car dealerships), Ingmire has become familiar with the various sales bonuses and incentives employed in the trade. He stresses that car salesmen are paid in different ways throughout the country. He explains how the system works in San Francisco, which is similar to how it operates in many other localities:

To begin with, a salesman is paid differently for selling a new car than for a used one. For a new car, the salesman gets 40 percent of the gross profit of the sale; for a used car, he gets 7 percent of the sticker price. For example, a new car that is sold for $5,000 may have cost the dealer $4,000. So the salesman would get 40 percent of the difference, or $400. In the case of a used car, the salesman would get 7 percent of the selling price, regardless of what the dealer paid for the car. Therefore, a used car that sold for $2,000 would earn the salesman $140.

Ingmire explains that because of the way dealers pay used car salesmen, they usually do not inform the salesmen how much the dealer paid for the car originally. For one thing, it does not make any difference to the salesman since he is being paid strictly on a percentage of the final sale price. But just as important, it could affect the salesman's morale if he were aware of the actual details of the profit involved.

Some salesmen even get involved in a game they call "Playhouse 90" based on this situation, according to Ingmire. He stresses that it matters little to the salesman whether a car sells for, say, $1,800 or $2,000 since the difference to him is only $14. What is important to the salesman is to make the sale, not to squeeze every last penny out of the customer.

Here's how Ingmire explains the "Playhouse 90" game: "Let's say a customer tells the salesman he is willing to buy a car for $1,800 even though the dealer's asking price is $2,000. What the salesman can do is to tell the customer to put down a bid of $1,600 on a sheet of paper, which the salesman then takes to the dealer. Then the salesman tells the dealer, 'Let me try to get him up to $1,800,' but does not tell the dealer the customer has already agreed to that figure. If the dealer agrees, the salesman knows he has a sale and nobody is any the wiser."

In addition to the standard sales commissions, Ingmire explains that car salesmen often receive a variety of bonuses. They can get extra money for selling a high number of cars in a certain month or "spiff bonuses," for selling cars that have been in stock for a long time, such as more than sixty or ninety days. They may get a bonus for selling a "Sally Ran" or "Plain Jane" — a car that has no options, such as a manual transmission, six-cylinder American car with no power steering and only a radio and heater. Finally, many dealers also give bonuses to salesmen who also get the customer to use the dealer's financing and/or insurance plans.

Ingmire does not have to worry about sales commissions since he runs a one-man operation at present. He realizes that a used car salesman has a few strikes against him that need to be overcome. "A lot of people are afraid of the used car salesman. On a scale of one to ten, he would probably be number nine, just above a politician. So I try to let people know that I'm not going to bite them, I'm not going to treat them wrongly. I'm just trying to help them buy a car."

To Ingmire, "I sell myself first. I certainly wouldn't buy something from somebody I don't like. So I try to get to know someone and I want them to know me. I'm not grouchy, and I do not drink. One of the things that turns me off when I'm a consumer, when I go in to buy a coat or something, is to have a salesperson walk up to me and I smell booze on their breath. If I don't like it, I assume other people don't like it, either. I try to be friendly; I just try to be me. Since I have an outgoing personality, I do a lot of kidding." (When I watched Ingmire in action one day, he once lifted a Chicano customer's leather cowboy hat off his head, put it on his own, and told the customer that he'd reduce the price of the car by $200 if he could keep the hat.)

One kind of customer Ingmire detests is the "tire kicker" – someone who is "just looking." He says, "One of my first questions is, 'Are you going to buy a car today? If I show you the right car, are you going to buy it?' " For those who cannot answer affirmatively, Ingmire tells them, "We sell cars here. We don't sell apples, bananas, or watermelons here. I'm trying to make my living selling cars here.

"Once we've got that out of the way, that the person is looking for a car, I try to find them the right car that fits their budget and needs. I ask what kind of work they do for a living and what kind of use they would have for a car. And I ask about how much they want to spend for the car. If they're interested in something less than $1,000, I don't show them a car worth $1,500 because that's wasting my time."

One of the aspects of selling used cars that bothers him the most is dealing with customers who later develop problems with their cars. "If you buy a used car from someone and something goes wrong with it, who do people blame? Not the car, but the salesman who sold it to them! I turn that right around, I say, 'I did not sell you the car, you *bought* it. Did I tell you this was the greatest car in the world? No, I told you it was a used car and that if it was perfect, the original owner would have it, not me."

Occasionally Ingmire's hard-nosed approach to dissatisfied customers has not worked. But he says he's only been sued twice in small claims court, and that he won one of those suits.

One time, however, an unhappy customer threatened his life after the car he bought had caught fire. "He blamed me for that and said it was my fault," Ingmire recalls. "He came in here and said, 'I can get you killed for $300.' He sat right there in that chair and said the going price to get someone rubbed out in this town is $300."

Ingmire says he did not even flinch. "I had to say to him, 'Hey, you're getting cheated because I can get you rubbed out for $150.' If I showed fear, if I were to immediately jump up and tell him I would do anything he wanted, the next thing I'd know I'd have to fix a flat tire. Once you fix something, there's no stopping. My policy is never to fix anything and let people know that when they take that car, they own it."

Roderick Leake — A Curbstoner

For the past seven years. Roderick Leake has earned a living selling automobiles. But except for a brief stint with a car dealership in Virginia, the people buying cars from him have not realized that he was in the car business. Leake calls himself a "curbstoner" – someone who buys and sells cars privately and keeps the profits as income.

Leake got started as a "curbstoner" while in graduate school in New Jersey during the early 1970s. When he was short of funds at one point, he decided to sell his aging Mercedes 190. He tacked up a notice on a school bulletin board that he was selling the car for $1,300, and the first fellow to take a look at the car bought it. "Since I bought the car two-and-a-half years earlier for $700, I said to myself, 'Wow, if I can make $600 on a car like this, I might as well get to work and start making some money in the used car business."

Since that time, Leake estimates he has sold about 120 autos on his own. "Next to real estate, it's probably the best way to make money fast – that's legal. I think the drug trade involves a lot more money than either the automobile trade or the real estate trade. But I've never been into that."

One of Leake's major concerns has been to maintain a low profile so as not to attract the attention of state law enforcers who prosecute those who deal in cars without the proper state licenses. "It's best to only do one car at a time," Leake says. "If you do too many, you have people calling you, saying, 'Hey, that car you have advertised in the paper. . . . If you respond, 'What car?' then right away people think you are dealing in automobiles."

A more ticklish problem is how to keep his name off the car registration papers. Leake explains his tactic: "You avoid the state by making sure the state doesn't know you are a party involved in the sale of the car. When you buy the car, you don't put your name on the title or registration papers."

What does Leake do when he sells the car? "If I bought a '64 Chevy from somebody named Samuel Jackson, his name would probably be on the registration. But let's say I were selling it to a man named Robert Thompson. He and I would come into my house and we would sit down and I'd say, 'O.K., Mr. Thompson, that car is $250. Give me the money.' Once the money is in my hand, I pull out the title and say, 'Sign your name right here, Mr. Thompson.' He'll usually just say, 'Thank you very much.'

"If you do it fast and you do it with verve, you have the party in your hand at all times. I make sure they sign their name and their address. I get their phone number. I fold up the title, give it back to them, and say, 'Have a good day. Enjoy your automobile.' As far as they know, I'm Samuel Jackson because they haven't even asked me my name because I keep them so busy all the time just talking about cars. I don't say what my name is because I don't want to misrepresent myself."

Leake's need to avoid the law has also meant he has had to go the extra mile to satisfy his customers. "I once sold a car to some people who called me three or four days later and told me the car had failed to pass state inspection because the alignment system was so messed up that the car wobbled. I could have contested it and refused to give them their money back. But by doing that I might arouse the ire of the purchasing party and they may go to the consumer complaint department of the motor vehicles bureau, who might come out and interview me or something. That would just cause more complications because I want to keep a low profile.

"So, believe it or not, there are a lot of used car people, who for their own protection, and out of the sake of integrity, deal with people legitimately. I realized in this case that it was my obligation to get those people squared away."

He explains how he solved this problem. "The way you square people away is what involves the ingenuity in the used car business. What I would try to do is have them buy another car that I had just picked up. That would save me the hassle of getting their car straightened out. Then I could pawn their car off to another party by advertising it as a car that needs mechanical work. Or I could take their car to a used car dealer that had a pile of junkers in the back and trade in their car for a better one and give the dealer about $100."

Aside from the legal problems of curbstoners, Leake says "The most important thing is to make sure you get a decent car when you buy one because it can mean a lot of complications to buy a car with mechanical defects." Leake finds the cars he buys through newspaper want-ads, and he always buys from private individuals rather than from used car dealers. He asks the owner over the phone how many miles are on the car, how long they have owned the car and whether it has any broken glass or any other mechanical problems. "Mostly I am interested in price because I want to be able to make a profit out of the car."

Once he has decided a car may be a good purchase, he goes to take a look at it at the owner's house. Before he even goes up to the house, he usually takes a look at the car on the street to check the tire wear, to see whether there are any cracks in the windshield, to find out if there are any obvious signs of rust, and to observe whether there are any holes in the muffler or if the exhaust pipes are properly connected. He does not even bother to knock on the owner's door if the car flunks this cursory inspection.

After he meets the owner, Leake says he insists on taking the car for a short test drive in which he is primarily interested in listening to the sound of the motor, how the transmission works, and how the brakes work ("Some people buy cars strictly on the condition of the brakes"). When he is also satisfied that the doors open and close satisfactorily and that the lights work ("electrical work is expensive"), Leake is ready to bargain.

"If I like the car, I usually go back into the owner's house and say, 'Well, the car has a few problems.' I don't inflate what the problems are, but believe me, I know what they are. Then I usually offer them about $25 less than what they are asking for the car. Everybody accepts that kind of offer on the spot. Then I try to find out what else is wrong with the car so that when I sell the car, I can tell the buyer what's wrong. I don't want them to come back at me saying that I am really a scam after they buy the car from me. It's not my art to mislead people.

It's my art to get the money I want for a car and to inform people what's wrong with it so they will be fairly well-satisfied that they made a good deal."

Leake normally spends a few hours getting the car into shape for sale. In terms of the mechanical items, he works on the:

- Radiator. Drains, flushes and puts in antifreeze, even in the summer since that is always a "selling point."
- Battery. Cleans both the battery and its cables and makes sure he has a "good start on the car."
- Oil. Makes sure the oil is topped off. "If the oil is extremely dirty, I'll take it out, and I might even put in a new oil filter if I can get a good buy on filters."
- Incidentals. "I make sure that all the lights work, the horn, the radio, fan – simple things. When people get in the car, I want everything to work. People would be more satisfied to pay $300 for a car where everything works than $75 for a car where they have to do a lot of these incidentals."

In addition to these minor mechanical tasks, Leake devotes some time to what he calls the "cosmetics." He says, "Cosmetics oftentimes sell a car, especially when a woman is involved. Most cars aren't pretty to begin with, so I make sure that the buying population understands that when I first talk to them on the phone. I get them in the mental framework that it's no gem but that it's not beat-up either. That way, when they come out, they are in the state of mind to accept the car."

Specifically, Leake explains, "I wash it, vacuum it, and usually put some cheap seat covers on it. It's always worth the five or six dollars for the seat covers." He also makes some effort to make the engine look clean, but he does not steam clean it. "The engine should not be perfectly clean on an older car. It's a giveaway to a buying party."

Finally, Leake explains, "If it is a newer model car, I usually park it to take advantage of the shade to hide one side that might be more faded or beat up than the other." But Leake generally stays away from newer cars. "When you put out more than a thousand for a car, you run into a more discriminating buying population. You have to bend over backwards to please them. They are not the immediate-type buyer that needs a car. They are only looking, and a looking population I can do without because I can't turn my money over fast enough."

Leake says that as a low-profile curbstoner he earns about $1,000 to $1,200 a month by selling only three or four cars during that time. He defends the practice. "Nowadays, somebody who operates like me can offer the public what I think is a better deal than a used car salesman. I can sell it much cheaper – about $300 less per car because I don't have their overhead. And with that $300, a buyer can get the car in tip-top shape."

Car Dealer Todd S. Cochran

Before becoming a co-owner of a Dodge dealership, Todd S. Cochran was a top auto salesman, selling nearly three hundred cars a year – almost one car a day! He says he learned the trade the hard way. Though he started working for a car dealership in the late 1940s, he was not permitted to sell cars because of racial discrimination. But because he worked in the new car showroom keeping the cars clean, Cochran overhead the white salesmen making their sales pitches to the customers: "I listened to them very carefully and heard quite a few mistakes. I would listen to the different lies the salespeople told."

But Cochran insists he has been more forthright in his dealings as a salesman: "My mother was an evangelist. When I told her that I was going to be a car salesman, she said, 'I hate to see you get into this business because it means you have to lie and misrepresent what you do.' But I told her, 'If the day comes when I have to lie to sell a car, I will get out of the business.' That has been my philosophy then and now."

As a car dealer, Cochran bemoans the amount of money he has to spend on advertising. He estimates that advertising costs $400 for every new car that is sold and between $100 and $150 for every used car.

"Beautiful Bob"

Bob White was nearly forty years old before he sold his first car, and that sale happened quite inadvertently. One day in 1964 he was waiting for his son to get off work at a car dealership in Southern California. Because his son was too busy to talk with all the customers in the waiting room, he asked his father to show a young couple a new car.

"But I don't know anything about cars," White protested. "It would be like the blind leading the blind." White also felt uneasy since he had never sold anything before in his life; he only recently had accepted early retirement from his job as a corporate attorney for a major oil company in Tulsa, Oklahoma.

White's son assured him that he needed no knowledge about cars to sell them, and then the son gently pushed his father toward the unsuspecting couple. No sooner had White walked onto the car lot with the potential customers than "I just fell in love with this car. They did, too, because I did, and they bought it on the spot."

For his efforts, White was paid $125, and he soon signed up to work as a car salesman himself, convinced the car business was an easy way to supplement his small early retirement allowance.

White's first car sales job was in a "T.O. house," which is also referred to as a "turnover house" or "turnover store." As opposed to a "straight sell store," where one salesman takes care of everything, a T.O. house uses several salesmen for each customer. When someone appears on the lot, a "liner" meets him. "A liner doesn't actually sell," White explains. "He's like a PR man basically, but he gets a percentage of the sale for customers he greets and talks with. He greets them and then he turns them over to somebody else who grinds them — that is, tries to get them to buy a car."

White said that in many cases a customer is "turned over" to more than one salesman. "They keep turning you over to different people until they have found a salesman who has gained your confidence. Let's face it, you would never buy a car from somebody if you had a personality clash with them, no matter what the price, the color, or whatever."

Soon after a customer has arrived on the lot, a liner or a salesman tries to get him to fill out a credit application. While the customer and a salesman continue amiably chatting about cars, unbeknownest to the customer the sales manager often has a thorough credit check done, using the Social Security number or other information the customer has provided.

"In the back room, they have a bank of computers going so that in fifteen minutes, with some of these new computer setups, they can tell you about the last bill you didn't pay, whether you paid last month's electric bill, and so on," White explains. "If they think you are good credit, they will concentrate on you. But if you're a bad credit risk or they think you're a flake, they'll fluff you off, get rid of you fast."

While the computers are whirring in the back room, the salesman tries to engage the customer in what is called the "red-lining" process. Here's how it works, according to White. "They put a blank order form in front of the customer and try to get him to put down how much he's willing to pay for the car. If they can get the customer's signature on it, he's hooked. At least that's the first hook. Any time you sign something, you think you've bought that car when you make that offer."

At this point, the salesman often leaves the customer alone in the salesman's office while he consults with his manager. Soon the salesman returns with a red line through the customer's offer on the order form and with a counter offer from the dealer in its place. This "redlining" game can go on for hours as the salesman shuttles back and forth from the customer to his manager. If the negotiations become too tense, the initial salesman may turn the customer over to another salesman, who sometimes is called the "manager" even if, in reality, he is only another salesman.

White says that some of these dealerships even "bug" the sales offices. "That way the sales managers can sit and listen to what the conversation is inside," explains White. Not only can the managers decide whether the salesman is maintaining his rapport with the customers but they can also listen to the private conversations of the customers themselves when the salesman is out of the room.

White gives an example of this in action: "Say a man and woman came in and have just made an offer of $5,000 on a redlining sheet for a certain car that the dealer has for sale at $6,000. While the salesman is out of the room, Annie is talking to George and says, 'Well what do you think? We can only go $5,500. That's our top dollar. Our payments would be atrocious on anything higher.'

"Remember, this is all being listened to by someone else – all the private conversation between these two people. Since they're getting the whole spiel in the back room, Annie and George don't have a chance. The manager knows exactly how to bargain since he knows all their personal business. He can just tell the salesman, 'They just said they can go up to $5,500.' At that point, the dealer has a weapon that can't be defeated."

White is quick to point out that bugging of offices is extremely rare these days and that most dealers are legitimate. He even says that some of the salesmen had no knowledge of what went on in the back room. "I was just as innocent when I started work in one of those T.O. houses in 1964. I didn't know about these things. You just sort of learn about them. Besides, the dumber the liners are, the better they are. They don't know what's going on in the back room. They don't even know sometimes that the offices are bugged."

Since his days as a liner in T.O. houses, White has worked at several dealerships selling new and used cars. In 1977 he set out on his own by buying his own used car lot, which he calls "Beautiful Bob's Auto Sales." He says, "We guarantee our cars around the world or around the block, whichever comes first."

His advice to prospective car buyers is simple: "Beware of anybody who advertises on TV and says that they are going to give you X number of dollars for your car, running or not. Let's face it: The public is dumb and the public is greedy, and a lot of these dealers play to that greed.

"After all, what's your first thought when you go out and look for a car? You think, 'I want to get something for the cheapest possible price.' Well, let's face it. Knowing economics and how much things cost, you don't get something for nothing, and anybody with any intelligence should know to avoid that particular pitfall. But the public's greed is what the whole TV ad business is aimed at. It's amazing how many people will go to those places and just throw themselves in the meat grinder of their own volition."

White asserts that "the ones that get hooked are the ones that are greedy in the first place. The ones that think they are going to save a thousand dollars will probably end up paying a thousand more than if they had been more cautious."

At the same time, White thinks many car shoppers are overly suspicious: "Some people go in with all the weapons it takes, like a copy of the Blue Book. But they're usually the ones that go without being able to buy a car at all because they are too tight, too cautious. You can't do that. You've got to realize that it costs so much to make the car, and you have to pay a commission to the salesman and pay for the overhead and give the dealer a fair profit."

11 Now that you've BOUGHT IT . . .

After all the time and effort you've presumably put into buying a good used car, you certainly will want to take some simple measures to take care of it.

CARING FOR YOUR CAR

Within the first few weeks of buying a used car, you should do the following:

1 Get a copy of the owner's manual if the car did not come with it. This booklet can tell you exactly what kind of maintenance routine the manufacturer prescribes for the car – such as its lubrication schedule. In addition, it gives you or your mechanic precise specifications for items like the proper spark plug gap. You can usually obtain an owner's manual from the parts department of a new car dealer. If the dealer doesn't have any in stock (which is often the case if you have an older used car), you can often buy a manual that has similar information from many auto parts stores. For

instance, Chilton puts out a series of paperback repair manuals for most models. You can write Chilton's Books, Radnor, Pennsylvania 19089, for a catalog.

2 Change the oil and oil filter. Few people bother with this task right before they sell their car. So it may have been many thousands of miles ago that the oil was last changed.

3 Get the car lubricated. Have the transmission and differential fluids checked and changed, if dirty.

4 Get at least a minor tune-up; that is, clean and gap the spark plugs, adjust the points and set the timing. If you think it's needed, have a full tune-up done, including replacing the plugs, points, condenser, PCV valve and adjusting the carburetor.

5 Get repairs done for the major problems uncovered during your prior inspection of the vehicle. For instance, if you learned that the brakes need to be relined, don't wait until they become a safety hazard. You should have already figured that you would have to sink some more money into the car when you purchased it – unless you were able to get the previous owner to make repairs for you. If you got the previous owner to reduce the price to accommodate repairs that you felt were needed, don't skimp on making the repairs now that you won the car yourself. It's always cheaper to fix something in a car before it breaks altogether.

If you have a warranty, you should pay particular attention to how the car behaves during the period covered by the warranty. Does it make any unusual sounds or noises you hadn't noticed before? Does it burn excessive amounts of oil? Does there seem to be a leak in the radiator? Are there problems when you drive it long distances? Remember that once the thirty-, sixty-, or ninety-day warranty period is over, it's *over*.

If you don't have a warranty or once the warranty period is over, don't mislead yourself into thinking that you can simply pour gas into your car and forget about it. Cars, particularly older ones, tend to be tempermental. They require constant love and attention. If neglected, they invariably break down and cost you lots of money.

For the first few weeks or so, I suggest you do the following whenever you fill up the gas tank:

1 Check the fluid levels of the oil, radiator water, battery acid, brakes, and, if you have them, automatic transmission and power steering. If you can't stand the idea of getting your hands dirty, have the service station attendant do it for you.

2 Check the tire pressure. A tire gauge costs less than $2 at most car parts stores and is well worth the investment. If you don't know how much air is supposed to be in your tires, call up a tire store or new car dealer repair department and ask. The tire size is clearly imprinted on the side of the tire.

After you've had the car a few weeks, you can gradually cut down on how frequently you check these items. But you should continue to monitor the oil and radiator fluid levels and the tire pressure every few weeks. The other fluids should be looked at at least once a month. I've heard countless stories from my mechanic friends about engines that have overheated and literally self-destructed merely because the owners hadn't noticed the low water or oil levels.

Getting Your Car Repaired

Simple maintenance can help you avoid some car problems — even serious ones — but car parts do wear out and stop working. Certain parts — like brakes, mufflers, clutches — won't normally last as long as the whole car. Hopefully, you won't need to have the entire engine replaced (though VW Beetle owners almost consider blown engines to be part of the bargain). At any rate, most used car owners can anticipate sending their cars to a repair shop from time to time.

Unfortunately, the typical motorist only has a 50-50 chance of getting his or her car fixed right at a fair price. At least that's what a recent federal Department of Transportation study disclosed. The DOT study also revealed that American drivers are overcharged an average of $150 per car per year.

The DOT conducted its survey by sending members of an undercover team to repair shops throughout the country with certain specific problems. For instance, five cars had one spark plug without a gap, causing the engine to misfire badly. Rather than correctly locating the problem and adjusting the spark plug gap, all of these repair facilities replaced all of the plugs and in some instances performed major tune-ups on the engines. The five garages charged a total of $426.91 for unnecessary work, according to the DOT.

The DOT's survey is not the only federal study that came to such a dismal conclusion about the chances of getting treated fairly by repair shops. In 1978 the National Highway Traffic Safety Administration produced a report which estimated that nearly 40 percent of the costs associated with auto repairs are excessive. That's a total annual loss to consumers of $20 billion out of the estimated $50 billion spent each year on car repairs.

Finding a Good Mechanic

You can save yourself lots of money and needless hassles by finding reliable and honest repair shops for your car. But there are so many auto mechanics and garages in most communities that making a good choice may seem like a hopelessly frustrating task.

Start by asking your friends about where they take their cars for repairs. Find out as much as you can about their mechanics. Inquire whether they fix problems properly, charge reasonable rates, offer written estimates in advance of working on the car, and give guarantees. Most important, would they recommend their mechanics or repair shops without qualification?

If you are lucky, you may learn of one or two good mechanics from your friends. But if you have to start from scratch, you might like to know some of the pluses and minuses of the four main types of repair shops: independent garages; new car dealerships; service stations; and speciality shops.

Independent Garages For major repair jobs, these shops often offer the most reliable work at the most reasonable prices. Many of the most highly qualified and experienced mechanics ply their trade in these shops. Frequently these mechanics graduated to these garages after years of work at new car dealerships or service stations. Some independent garages specialize in certain makes of cars or specific types of repairs. Because these garages rely on the reputation they acquire in a community, they often make special efforts to make sure they fix problems well.

Two drawbacks. Some of these operations are quite small, with one or two mechanics, which may make them slower than some of the higher volume shops. Also, these garages can cost more for common repair problems that don't really require the touch of an expert — such as a simple brake job, muffler installation, oil change, and lubrication.

New Car Dealerships Since these garages are affiliated with manufacturing firms, their mechanics often become extremely familiar with the problems of certain models. On the other hand, they often charge higher rates for labor and parts than many independent garages, so that on the average these are the most expensive places for repairs.

Service Stations Some extremely talented mechanics work in service station garages, but many novices also work in these shops. Unless you know for sure that a service station mechanic is a pro, you should avoid using these garages for major repair jobs. Nevertheless, these shops can usually perform simple maintenance tasks, such as oil changes and lubrications, as effectively and more cheaply than the other options. Some of these garages are also quite good at somewhat more complicated jobs like repairing or replacing brakes, mufflers, shock absorbers, and doing tune-ups. Try to avoid service stations garages where the mechanics also pump gas.

Specialty Shops Included in this category are franchise operations like AAMCO Transmission and Midas Mufflers, mass merchandisers like Sears and J. C. Penney, and franchise repair shops affiliated with national tire companies like Goodyear and Firestone. The high volume of their specialty work makes it possible for these companies to offer cheaper rates for certain kinds of repairs. Like service stations, these garages are rarely where you should go for a major auto repair, such as an engine overhaul, and they don't do general diagnostic work. However, they often do competent work on the jobs they perform regu-

Fix-It-Yourself Mechanic Bill Crowe

larly. A word to the wise: Be sure you know precisely what your car needs before going to one of these specialty shops. They are in the business of selling a certain product and will tend to give it to you regardless.

Certified Mechanics and Garages

Many states have regulations for car repair facilities. In such places, the repair shops must abide by certain disclosure procedures when dealing with their customers. Sometimes that means that the shop must give written estimates, return replaced parts, and refrain from certain deceptive practices, such as charging for work that was not performed. Before 1973, only three states had laws regulating auto repair garages, but by 1979, twenty-one states and the District of Columbia had such laws.

If you are lucky enough to live in one of those places, familiarize yourself with the consumer protections provided by the law. You can usually get that information directly from the certified garages or from a local state office of consumer affairs.

In some other locations, the American Automobile Association chapter maintains an Approved Auto Repair program to rate auto repair shops. These now exist in parts of Texas, Florida, Southern California, and Washington, D.C. and the AAA hopes to expand this program to other communities.

A consumer group in the District of Columbia conducted a survey of repair shops in the metropolitan area and published the results of their inquiry. It is willing to help other consumer groups interested in conducting similar surveys in their communities. If interested, write the Washington Center for the Study of Consumer Services, 1518 K Street, N.W., Suite 406, Washington, D.C. 20005, and enclose $3 for costs.

As of 1978 only three states provide official certification for auto mechanics. But in 1972 an industry group called the National Institute for Automotive Service Excellence responded to the frequent criticisms of the profession by establishing qualifying tests for mechanics in various areas of auto repair. By 1978, NIASE had certified nearly 125,000 mechanics across the country.

You can obtain a free copy of a list of the auto repair shops which have NIASE-certified mechanics in your state by sending a self-addressed and stamped envelope to NIASE, 1825 K Street N.W., Washington, D.C. 20006. You can also receive a copy of their booklet containing a national directory of shops with NIASE mechanics by sending $1.95 to the same address.

These NIASE mechanics are not necessarily the best mechanics in your community, but you should expect a certain minimum standard of quality from their work.

Common Repair Rip-Offs

Unnecessary Repairs Garages sometimes try to convince you that a major repair is needed when a minor one would be sufficient. They may use scare tactics to convince you of the desirability of these unneeded repairs.

Phony Repairs Sometimes garages charge for repairs that weren't made or services that were not performed, or charge for new parts when secondhand or rebuilt parts were used. One example is "silver streaking" of a transmission, where you are told a new or rebuilt transmission has been installed when actually the bottom of the old one has been sprayed with silver paint – at a cost to you of several hundred dollars.

Bait and Switch You get lured into the shop because of its promise to provide a repair at a low price, then the garage tries to sell you on a more costly repair. For instance, you decide to go to a certain repair shop that advertised a $39.95 brake special, and when you get there you are told that that price only covers installing the new brakes – removing the old ones will cost you another $39.95.

Low-Balling The shop deliberately estimates a repair at an artifically low figure. Then when you come to pick up your car, you discover that the garage has escalated the costs and expects you to pay for the full amount.

Performing Unauthorized Repairs A friend of mine recently had a tune-up performed on his car. He agreed to a replacement of the points, plugs, and condenser. When he returned to pick up his car, he learned that the shop had also replaced his air filter and gas filter, charging him an extra $25 for parts and labor. Since he had put in these two parts himself only two weeks earlier, he demanded that they remove their new parts and reinstall his own – at no extra charge.

How to Deal with Your Mechanic

There are several steps you can take to avoid these and other typical repair shop abuses:

1. Know your mechanic. It's best to cultivate a relationship with a mechanic who has provided you with good work in the past. When you patronize someone frequently, he is less likely to take advantage of you since he won't want to lose your business. If you get burnt by a garage and don't get a satisfactory resolution of the problem, go somewhere else next time.

2. Describe symptoms, don't make prescriptions. When you go to a garage, tell the mechanic explicitly what is wrong with the car. Give details about how long the problem has existed, when you noticed it, what it sounds like, how it keeps the car from behaving normally. Unless you are 125 percent certain of what the problem is, you should let the mechanic make his own diagnosis. That is what you are paying him for.

Here's an example of why you should not normally tell the mechanic what repairs to make (unless you are merely requesting some kind of routine maintenance work, like a tune-up or oil change). My friend Edward recently found that his Toyota was slipping as he was going up steep hills. He assumed that the car needed a new clutch – a job that costs a minimum of $125. But when he went to his mechanic, he merely described the problem – how the car behaved climbing hills. Edward authorized only a diagnostic fee of $15. When the mechanic checked out the car, he discovered that the problem could be rectified by a simple adjustment of the clutch linkage and did not charge Edward any extra money.

Had Edward gone to the same garage and insisted that he wanted a new clutch, the mechanic probably would have installed a new clutch for $125 plus. Even if the garage had tried to determine whether an adjustment would be sufficient, Edward's instruction to replace the clutch could have created an unnecessary complication for the mechanic. The mechanic could easily have said to himself, "Maybe Edward wants a new clutch anyway. After all, the old one is somewhat worn. Anyway, it's his money, not mine."

3. Ask for old parts. Before the garage begins work on a job, ask that they return the old parts to you. That is the easiest way to protect yourself from phony repairs.

4. Obtain a written estimate in advance. Make sure you understand exactly what the garage intends to do to your car beforehand. When they give you an estimate, ask that they put it in writing. Above all, make sure they do not exceed their initial estimate of costs without your authorization. Low-balling is exceedingly common.

5. Never sign a blank work order.

6. Obtain several estimates. For a major repair, make sure that the repair is needed by getting more than one diagnosis of the problem. Once you are certain that the car requires the work, call up several garages to get their estimates. Be careful not to run off to the shop with the lowest price, however, especially if it sounds too low for the job. Make sure a garage offering an extremely low estimate is reputable and that you won't get involved in a "bait-and-switch" scam.

7. Demand an itemized invoice. When you pick up your car, ask that you get a list of the cost of each of the replacement parts and of the labor charges. This written invoice could be extremely important in case you must complain.

8. Get written guarantees. Don't assume that a garage will stand behind a mechanic's off-hand comment that "Your brakes will last for six months." If it's not in writing, the guarantee doesn't exist.

9. Complain if not satisfied. Approach the service manager with your complaint and try to get the matter resolved with him first. If that does not work, send the manager a letter detailing your complaint, specifying a time limit for his response. If the garage is part of a national or regional company, send a similar letter to the next higher levels in the company. If that fails, contact the local office of the state department of consumer affairs, phone the Better Business Bureau, or file a claim in small claims court.

10. Learn how cars work. Finally, your best protection against auto repair rip-offs is to become more informed about cars yourself. If you don't have any interest in getting your fingers greasy, you can read about the subject. Though I have not found any book that is a great introduction to the subject, I would recommend the following: *Everything I Know About Cars—Would Just About Fill A Book*, by Stephanie Judy, published in 1975 by Berkley Winhover Books, 200 Madison Avenue, New York, New York 10016. Judy has written a readable explanation of how a car works and how to maintain it.

For the more adventurous, you might consider taking a short course in auto mechanics. Such courses are commonly offered by many adult education programs and by some garages. You won't be able to do an engine overhaul after six weeks, but you probably won't look blankly at a mechanic who tells you your car needs a valve job.

I also recommend cultivating friends who are knowledgeable about cars. They can be helpful not only in avoiding problems with mechanics, but they can often teach you how to do relatively simple jobs like tune-ups or brake jobs.

If you want to teach yourself how to do your own car repairs, I recommend four books:

Chilton's Easy Car Care, available from Chilton's Books, Radnor, Pennsylvania 19089, as well as from many car parts stores. This gives a good introduction to how to perform simple repair jobs yourself. Chilton's also publishes a series of manuals for specific makes and models that can tell you more precisely how to repair problems with specific vehicles.

Petersen's Basic Auto Repair Manual, published by Petersen Publishing Company, 8490 Sunset Boulevard, Los Angeles 90069. This is a somewhat more complex book than the Chilton introductory book. I used it when I replaced a clutch on my old Dodge Dart.

How to Keep Your Volkswagen Alive, by John Muir, Box 613, Santa Fe, New Mexico 87501. Though written specifically for VW owners, this manual gives a highly amusing and accurate explanation of the workings of an automobile.

The Backyard Mechanic (Volumes I and II). Available from the federal government's Consumer Information Center, Pueblo, Colorado 81009. These two pamphlets give clear accounts of how to perform most simple maintenance and repair jobs.

INSURING YOUR CAR

It's a rare American who doesn't become "the other guy" at some point in his driving career. According to insurance industry statistics, the annual collision frequency rate is about 10.7 per 100 cars. Those same sources report that the average motorist will be involved in an accident twice during an eight-year period, and one of the accidents probably will be his or her fault.

In the face of such statistics, it seems foolish not to carry at least a minimal level of auto insurance. Of course, many states require car owners to insure their vehicles. But even in states without compulsory auto insurance, drivers can be held legally and financially accountable for damage caused by their cars.

What follows are a number of tips about auto insurance:

Shop around! Most people do absolutely no comparison shopping before choosing an auto insurance company. In fact, nearly three-quarters of all car insurance policyholders only consider one company, according to a 1975 Kemper Insurance Company survey.

Why don't people spend an extra few minutes on the phone? It certainly is not because all the insurance companies charge the same rates. On the contrary, auto insurance rates can vary so much that a driver could insure the same car with an identical policy for one-half or one-third as much with a different company.

Consumer Action, a California consumer group, surveyed the auto insurance rates of fourteen different companies in 1976. In its published report, Consumer Action disclosed the extent of the variations in insurance rates. For instance, a 35-year-old single woman living in a large city could be charged between $158 and $543 for identical 25/50/10 liability insurance policies for her '72 Chevrolet Nova. (See below for a definition of common auto insurance terms, a 25/50/10 liability policy.)

Decide in advance how much coverage you need. Don't forget that insurance agents and brokers are salespeople, many of whom are paid commissions on a percentage of the amount of the premiums they write. (The premium is the amount you pay the insurance company for your coverage.) So it is to their advantage for you to buy as much insurance as possible. This is another reason why you should check around with different companies to understand what is available before you make any commitments for insurance.

Obtain as much auto liability coverage as you can pay for. Premiums are only slightly higher for considerably greater levels of liability coverage. In the example cited above, the same company that provided 25/50/10 liability coverage for $158 also offered more than four times as much coverage — 100/300/25 — for an additional $32. If necessary, reduce your collision or comprehensive coverage by raising their deductibles to increase your liability coverage above a minimum level. Costs arising from serious accidents are usually much greater than minimum liability insurance can absorb.

Drop collision coverage when you can afford to replace the car yourself. Some insurance experts suggest that you should drop collision coverage when your car's wholesale (low Blue Book) value falls below $750, while others say you should consider eliminating it when your car is worth less than $1,000. Regardless, collision insurance is an expensive gamble. In my case, a $100 deductible collision premium is about $160 a year. I know that $160 is not much to protect a $2,000 car in case it were totalled in an accident. But if my car were valued at only $600, it would be far wiser not to carry any collision insurance at all. Even looking at such a situation superficially, it's obvious that $160 in collision insurance premiums alone would pay for a replacement vehicle in a few years.

Steer clear of insurance companies with bad reputations. If you know of friends or relatives who have had difficulty collecting claims or have experienced other problems with a specific insurance company, you should avoid it. Consumers Union rates the quality of services of auto insurance companies in its annual December buying guide of Consumer Reports magazines ($3 from Consumer Reports, Orangeburg, New York 10962).

Types of Auto Insurance Coverage

1. Liability You can cause thousands of dollars worth of damage with your car in an accident — both physical injuries or death to other people and destruction of other cars and property. By law, you can be forced to compensate others for that damage if you are held to be responsible for causing the accident. When you buy liability coverage, your insurance company agrees to pay *others* for accident damages when you are required to pay them. By obtaining this coverage, you also protect yourself — your own income, savings, and property.

2. Split-Limit Coverage Most insurance companies use an abbreviated form to express the maximum limits of liability coverage. For instance, a policy with a 25/50/10 limit means that the insurance company could have to pay up to $25,000 for one person injured or killed and a maximum of $50,000 for all people injured or killed in an accident. The third figure of the 25/50/10 example signifies that the company could be liable for a maximum of $10,000 in property damages from an accident.

3. Single-Limit Coverage. Some companies also offer a plan that states a maximum amount that can be paid for all damages — to both persons and property — from a single accident, with $300,000 for any combination of damages to one or more persons and vehicles.

4. Medical Payments This is like your own personal medical insurance policy to cover hospital and doctor bills for you or your passengers in case of an accident, regardless of fault. You won't need this coverage if you already have an adequate medical insurance policy.

5. Uninsured Motorist This covers you in case someone else is at fault in an accident but doesn't have any liability insurance. It's generally worth carrying this coverage, especially in states that don't require all drivers to carry liability insurance.

6. Emergency Road Service and Towing. Similar to the service provided by auto clubs, such as AAA, but often much cheaper. For instance, I pay about $7 a year for this coverage from my insurance company (State Farm), while the local AAA charges about $25 for its annual membership.

7. Medical Payments Similar to your own personal medical insurance policy. Your hospital and doctor bills are covered for you or your passengers in case of an accident, regardless of fault.

8. Collision Covers the cost of repairs to your vehicle in case of an accident, even if you were responsible for the accident. If you buy collision, remember that the premium decreases markedly with a higher *deductible*. In other words, if your deductible is $100, the insurance company will only have to pay for repair damages in excess of that amount. So if your car is involved in an accident that caused your car $550 worth of damage, you would have to pay $100 and the insurance company would pay the $450 balance. With a $250 deductible, you would have to pay $250; the insurance company $300. Consequently, your collision insurance premium would be much lower for a $250 deductible than a $100 deductible. It's generally a good idea to increase the deductible as a car gets older, and to drop collision coverage altogether when a car drops below about $1,000 in value.

9. Comprehensive Covers repair damages to your car in case of theft, vandalism, fire, or storm damage. Like collision, your premium for this coverage decreases with a higher deductible.

10. Premium The amount you pay the insurance company for the types of coverage you elect to purchase. These rates vary according to the car owner's age, sex, driving record, and place of residence. Also, bigger and sportier cars are usually more expensive to insure than smaller and more sedate models; and it's cheaper to insure a car used for personal pleasure than for business. Cars used less than 7,500 miles a year can also usually be insured at a lower premium rate.

Auto insurance rates are based on your age, sex, driving record, where you live, your car's value, and whether you use the car for business or pleasure. Although the insurance industry is highly regulated in most states, the rates vary widely among various companies. By phoning different auto insurance companies, you'll quickly discover variations of $100 or more in annual premium rates for the same policy coverage.

Again, as with anything else related to cars, it pays to use the phone to *shop around* before committing yourself.

Although liability insurance varies somewhat in states with "no-fault" insurance plans, you probably will need it anyway. You can still be sued in those states if someone claims damages above their "personal injury" limits, and you would be unprotected without liability coverage.

12 Fighting the GAS CRISIS

It seems that we are constantly surrounded by a multitude of competing facts, figures, and explanations of the gas crisis. But little accurate or useful information ever manages to reach most motorists about how to cope with the indisputable reality — the rising cost of gasoline at service station pumps.

For instance, most car owners do *not* realize that:

1 A motorist who is getting only 10 mpg from his car can offset a whopping 20¢ per gallon gas price hike by bettering his car's mileage to 12 mpg;

2 Improving a car's gas mileage from 28 to 30 mpg makes significantly less difference in a driver's annual fuel costs than an advance from 18 mpg to 20 mpg;

3 A motorist's driving habits and techniques can have a greater impact on gas mileage than vehicle design.

At the end of this chapter, I provide a list of twelve tips on how to improve your car's gas mileage and reduce your annual auto fuel expenses. A few of these tips may sound familiar since variations of some of these ideas – such as driving less than 55 mph – have already become part of the American motoring consciousness.

Before I throw out my full list of pointers, let's consider some of the factors that contribute to your car's gas bills. To begin, I should underscore that *by improving you car's gas mileage, you can often neutralize a big increase in the price of gasoline.*

Look at Table 12.1, which illustrates this point in stark monetary terms. You can see, for instance, the effect of bettering gas mileage from 10 mpg to 12 mpg. Not only does that 2 mpg difference offset a 20¢ per gallon hike in gas prices, but the chart also shows that a driver can make up for a huge 40¢ per gallon jump at the pumps by upping his or her car's gas mileage from 10 mpg to 14 mpg.

One other figure to note from the same chart. Look at what $500 in annual fuel costs represents. As you can see, improvements of 2 mpg from 18 mpg to 20 mpg can compensate for a 10¢ per gallon increase in the price of gas.

You may have noticed an extremely important point about gas costs from the two examples I have cited or from a careful examination of the same annual fuel costs chart (Table 12.1): *THE MOST SIGNIFICANT IMPROVEMENTS IN GAS SAVINGS OCCUR AT GAS MILEAGE RATES BELOW RATHER THAN ABOVE 20 MPG.*

To dramatize this all-important fact about gas mileage, I have produced a graph (Table 12.2). You can see at a glance the steepness of the line representing annual fuel costs at the lower gas mileage rates. This means that even a small improvement in your car's mpg can have a big impact on your gas bill. By contrast, the graph line begins to level off after about 20 mpg and becomes nearly horizontal after 30 mpg.

Consider this example from the graph: At $1 a gallon, there's a $250 savings between 8 mpg and 10 mpg – a difference of only 2 mpg. But it takes a jump from 20 mpg to 40 mpg – ten times the 2 mpg – to obtain the same $250 savings.

Put in other terms, you don't need to be bowled over by the high gas mileage ratings boasted by some car makers. The people who rushed out to put their names on waiting lists for diesel-powered VW Rabbits don't realize that they will probably never save enough in their gas costs to offset the extra hundreds or thousands of dollars they spent to get a car that is supposed to get an EPA combined estimate of 40 mpg.

By the same token, it makes a big difference in your annual fuel costs to get 15 mpg rather than 10 mpg, or 20 mpg rather than 15 mpg.

For the more mathematically inclined readers: The reason for the relative differences at various gas mileage rates is simple. It is based on the formula used to determine annual fuel costs:

$$\frac{\text{Total miles driven}}{\text{Miles per gallon (mpg)}} \quad \text{X} \quad \text{Price per gallon} = \text{Annual gas costs}$$

So, for example, to determine how much it would cost to drive a car that averages 20 mpg for 10,000 at $1 per gallon:

$$\frac{10{,}000 \text{ miles}}{20 \text{ mpg}} \times 1 = \$500$$

"Your Actual Mileage May Differ . . ."

Just to rub the point in for your diesel-Rabbit-owner friends, I should expand on that little proviso that is always included in advertisements of new car gas mileage estimates. You've undoubtedly heard TV commercial announcers state proudly that such-and-such a car gets a combined EPA estimate of, say, 28 mpg, but then add in a low voice, "Your actual mileage may differ, depending on your driving habits . . ."

What an understatement! Your driving habits can have an incredible impact on your gas mileage – so much so that, in some instances, you can almost forget the original EPA estimates.

How much of an impact? Consider this quote from a detailed study of fuel economy, published by the EPA "Driving habits and trip characteristics can have more effect on fuel economy than any vehicle design feature. A standard size car can get over 20 miles per gallon under favorable conditions; it can also get less than 2 miles per gallon under poor conditions."

What are some of these "driving habits and trip characteristics?" According to studies conducted by the EPA, the Federal Energy Administration, and the Department of Transportation, a car that can get approximately 20 mpg can lose the following:

- 2 mpg from "jackrabbit" starts and jerky acceleration;
- 1.3 mpg by "see-sawing" or repeatedly varying speed by 5 miles per hour;
- 2.5 mpg by using an air conditioner;
- 1 to 12 mpg by frequent, short trips from cold starts rather than combining trips or making only longer ones (see below);
- 3.5 mpg by driving at 70 mpg rather than 50 mph;
- 1.5 mpg when you drive in 20-degree weather as opposed to 70-degree weather;
- 2 mpg from driving in rain or snow;
- 2 mpg from driving into an 18 mpg headwind (or a 2.4 mpg gain from driving with an 18 mpg tailwind);
- 0.2 mpg from driving with an 18 mpg crosswind;
- 2 to 6 mpg from travel on rough or loose road surfaces such as sand or gravel.

The greatest variable in personal driving habits noted above is mileage loss due to short trips. Since the most frequently made car trip is about one mile long, the issue is particularly relevant for most car users. In fact, trips of five miles or less represent only about 15 percent of all miles traveled by American drivers each year, but such trips consume more than 30 percent of all auto fuel, according to the EPA.

The EPA suggests four reasons for the improvement of fuel economy as cars warm up on longer trips:

1 As the tires warm up and their inflation pressures rise, rolling friction decreases;

2 Engine and transmission friction decrease as the lubricants become warmer;

3 The engine's carburetion gets leaner (less gas, more air) as the engine heats up; and

4 After the combustion chamber walls and coolants warm up, less combustion heat is lost.

Gas Lines, Summer 1979

Most of the public discussion of the causes of the gas lines that plagued American motorists in 1973-74 and again in 1979 has centered on gasoline shortages. Blame has been assigned variously to the Arabs, the big oil companies, the bungling U.S. Department of Energy, Detroit's gas-guzzling autos, and the fuel-wasting habits of American drivers.

Often overlooked in this discussion has been the huge increase in the number of automobiles on the road in the recent past. For instance, there are more than twice as many cars now as there were just twenty years ago. In 1958 there were 56 million cars compared with 113 million registered automobiles by the beginning of 1978. Translated into other terms, that means that while there was only one car for every three people (including children) in 1958, today there is one car for every two people in the total population of about 220 million. That figure is even lower when you include the more than thirty million trucks and buses and five million motorcycles also on the American highways competing for automotive fuels.

Some more facts to underscore this point. There has been a net increase of between two and three million automobiles *every year* since the late 1950s. Much of this increase can be attributed to the millions of new cars produced annually. In 1978 there were nearly eleven million new cars purchased in this country as opposed to only six million in 1959.

One other fact to keep in mind when sitting in a gas line: the typical American motorist drives his car 9,634 miles per year, consumes 712 gallons of gasoline, and gets 13.53 miles per gallon.

As a result of these factors, fuel economy drops drastically on shorter trips made from cold starts. Based on the EPA's findings of how many trips "a typical family car" can make on 25 gallons of gas, I have compiled the following chart:

Keep this chart in mind next time you're tempted to hop in your car for a quick trip to the corner store.

Return again to the list of factors that can affect loss in gas mileage. Except for the weather, most of the other causes stated earlier are well within our abilities to change. Just to stress again the importance of these driving habits, here is a telling quotation from an FEA pamphlet on the subject:

"The most important single element in determining the fuel economy of a particular car is the driving technique of the individual behind the wheel. One authority declares that a careful driver should be able to get at least 30 percent better mileage than an average one, and 50 percent better mileage than a poor one."

Take another glance at Table 12.1 in case you have difficulty adding up what a difference of 30 percent or 50 percent means in dollars and cents. Instead of a "poor" driver's 12 mpg, an "average one" could be getting nearly 16 mpg, while a "careful driver" could obtain 18 mpg. That's an annual difference, at $1 per gallon, of almost $200 and exactly $275 respectively!

Car Maintenance and Gas Consumption

Although not as significant a factor as your own driving habits, maintaining your car can influence your gas mileage significantly. Using the same federal pamphlets as above here are some of the gas economy losses that poor maintenance can cause:

- 0.6 to 1.8 mpg for an improperly tuned engine;
- 0.5 to 1.0 mpg for using regular tires rather than radial tires;
- 0.3 mpg from improper front wheel toe-in alignment;
- 0.2 mpg for each additional 100 pounds of extra weight; and
- up to 1.4 mpg for underinflated tires.

The government's estimates of the possible mileage increase from tune-ups may be too low. When I last did a complete tune-up on my car, I found the car getting an increase of about 3 mpg. I have other friends who say they've upped their gas mileage as much as 5 mpg after a major tune-up. I also know people who observed no immediate impact on their gas mileage, so you can't expect miracles every time.

Keep Your Own Gas Records

It's not difficult to keep track of your gas consumption. All you need is a working odometer on your car plus some kind of booklet to write down the information. I use a small spiral memo notebook, which I keep in the glove compartment of the car.

To begin, you need to write down the reading on your car's odometer (numbers of miles traveled) when you fill up the gas tank. (You can ignore the number of gallons from your first fill-up for these purposes.) The next time you get your car filled with gas, write down both the odometer reading and the number of gallons. To determine your gas mileage, you only need to subtract the second odometer reader from the first one and then divide that figure by the number of gallons you've used.

Here's an example from my Datsun B-210 notebook:

Date	*Mileage*	*Gallons*
6/11	51,321	8.2
6/21	51,533	9.5

On another page, I scribbled out the simple math involved:

	51,533
minus	51,321
equals	213 miles
divided by	9.5 gallons
equals	22.3 miles per gallon.

That was a slightly below-average week of stop-and-go city driving in my car. I get closer to 30 mpg when I make a number of highway trips between fill-ups, and over 30 mpg when I take long road trips. I've never come close to the advertised EPA estimate of 40 mpg on the highway for the B-210, nor is my average city mileage normally near the EPA estimate of 29 mpg. I attribute my car's relatively poor showing to the fact that the vast majority of my normal city driving is done in extremely congested areas of the city where there are stop signs or traffic lights on almost every block. What's more, many of my trips are from one to one-and-a-half miles long — all of which demonstrates the significance of the discussion above about short trips and gas mileage.

If nothing else, it's a good idea to keep track of your gas mileage to be aware of how much you're spending on gas. But it can also tip off any major problems with your car's engine if you discover a sudden drop in your car's gas mileage.

Gas-Saving Cars

Even a well-maintained '74 Lincoln Continental driven by the most gas-conscious Scotsman is unlikely to get better gas mileage than an overloaded, out-of-tune '80 Honda Civic CVCC with underinflated and poorly aligned, regular bias-ply tires driven by a hot rod dragster. Every car has its gas mileage limits determined mostly by its basic size and shape.

In comparing the Lincoln with the Honda, it should be noted that the Lincoln weighs more than three times the Honda (about 5,400 pounds versus about 1,800 pounds) and the Lincoln's engine is more than five times as big (its displacement is 460 cubic inches versus only 91 cubic inches for the Honda). According to the EPA, "The most important vehicle design features affecting fuel economy are vehicle weight and engine displacement. A 10 percent change in either weight or displacement causes a fuel economy change of 3 to 6 percent."

That's why smaller cars normally get better gas mileage. Other factors that improve gas mileage are manual transmission rather than automatic transmission (usually 1 to 3 mpg difference), and a smaller number of engine cylinders (four typically is better than six, which is better than eight).

The EPA's mileage estimates for newer cars unfortunately won't give most used car buyers a clear idea of what they should expect from many models of cars. In case you're interested in the EPA estimates for almost all new cars, you can get a free copy of EPA's "Gas Mileage Guide" by requesting it from:

Fuel Economy
Consumer Information Center
Pueblo, Colorado 81009.

Be sure to specify if you want the EPA's results for California cars since that state's emission control laws mean their cars get slightly different estimates.

On the subject of emission control laws: Don't think you can get better gas mileage by simply unhooking your car's emission control devices. In the first place, it's against a 1977 federal law for any service repair shop to tamper with such devices (a $2,500 fine), and most state laws also prohibit an individual car owner from disconnecting his or her car's pollution controls.

Even more relevant, you shouldn't assume that you can improve gas mileage by fiddling with the emission control system. Several extensive EPA studies have shown that most efforts, even by highly trained mechanics, don't increase gas mileage, and, in many cases, actually reduce it. This is particularly true of cars built since 1975 which have a complicated catalytic converter apparatus. Finally, it's easy to screw up your engine by altering these devices, and it may cost you more money in the long run to fix them.

Gas-Saving Tips

Plan Ahead! As you can see from the earlier discussion about how wasteful short trips can be, it pays to plan your driving in advance to combine errands whenever possible. In addition, make an effort to walk, use mass transit, or join car pools when you can. When you drive, think ahead to find the shortest routes and to avoid hills.

Drive Consistently! Keep a steady foot on the accelerator and avoid varying the speeds at which you drive. Don't adopt bad habits like constantly changing lanes. When you start from a stop, push down gently on the gas pedal. When you see a traffic light ahead turn red, let up on the accelerator immediately so you can coast rather than continue to use unneeded fuel. In traffic, avoid unnecessary braking by anticipating situations. Don't tailgate.

Slow Down! According to the FEA, most cars get about 28 percent more miles per gallon at 50 mph than at 70 mph, and about 21 percent better gas mileage at 55 mph than at 70 mph.

Drive in Higher Gears! Cars use more gas in lower gears. With a manual transmission, you save the most gas by moving steadily but quickly into high gear where you can gradually increase your speed. With an automatic transmission, you should hit the gas pedal just enough to get moving then let up slightly so the transmission moves into higher gears more readily.

Avoid Idling! It's cheaper to shut off and then restart your engine than to let it idle for more than one minute. Remember that fact when you're sitting in your car waiting for a friend, in a traffic jam, or in a gas line.

Avoid Using the Air Conditioner! The 2½ mpg loss using it adds up. In the course of a year, that could mean about $70 more in your gas bill (if your car gets about 20 mpg otherwise during a $1 per gallon/10,000-mile year).

Keep Your Engine Well-Tuned! Most car owner manuals advise a full tune-up every 10,000 miles, including changing spark plugs, points, condensers, PCV valve, air and gas filters. Make sure you or your mechanic set the timing and adjust the carburetor. You should also have the idle speed screw set as low as possible so you don't waste gas needlessly. It pays to do a mini-tune-up between major ones, such as every 5,000 miles, to clean the plugs and adjust the points and timing. You may save the price of such simple maintenance not only by lower gas costs but also by smaller repair bills in the long run.

Check Your Tires! You should use your tire gauge at least once a month to make sure your tires are not underinflated – a common gas-wasting habit. Also, radial tires not only save money for gas, but their slightly higher initial cost is offset by the generally longer tread wear.

Change Your Oil Regularly! Increased engine friction from dirty oil can cause poorer gas mileage as well as reduce engine life. Whatever your owner's manual states, you should probably change the oil more frequently, especially for older used cars. For the best gas mileage, you should use higher quality multi-grade oils (those that state 10W-30 or 10W-40, as opposed to those that have only one SAE number like 30).

Shop Around for Gas! Table 12.3 shows how much money you can save in a year by buying gas at 1¢ to 10¢ less. Since gas with lower octane ratings is also usually cheaper, you should determine the lowest octane your car can handle – that is, the lowest octane it can drive on without knocking – and use it.

Buy a Smaller Car! When you purchase a car, get the smallest one that will fit your needs. Cars that weigh less, have smaller engines, have fewer cylinders, and have manual transmissions generally get better gas mileage than their larger counterparts.

Keep Records! It's not only a way to make a running check of your own driving habits, but it can warn you of serious mechanical problems in advance.

Table 12.1 Annual Fuel Costs (10,000 miles*)

Average price per gallon

Gas mileage	90¢	$1.00	$1.10	$1.20	$1.30	$1.40	$1.50	$1.60	$1.70	$1.80	$1.90	$2.00
8 mpg	$1125	1250	1375	1500	1625	1750	1875	2000	2125	2250	2375	2500
10 mpg	900	1000	1100	1200	1300	1400	1500	1600	1700	1800	1900	2000
12 mpg	750	833	917	1000	1083	1167	1250	1333	1417	1500	1583	1667
14 mpg	643	714	786	857	929	1000	1071	1143	1071	1143	1214	1286
16 mpg	563	625	688	750	813	875	938	1000	1063	1125	1188	1250
18 mpg	500	556	611	667	722	778	833	889	944	1000	1056	1111
20 mpg	450	500	550	600	650	700	750	800	850	900	950	1000
22 mpg	410	455	500	545	591	636	682	727	773	818	864	909
24 mpg	375	417	458	500	542	583	625	667	708	750	792	833
26 mpg	347	385	423	462	500	538	577	615	654	692	731	769
28 mpg	321	357	393	429	464	500	536	571	607	643	679	714
30 mpg	300	333	367	400	433	467	500	533	567	600	633	667
32 mpg	282	313	344	375	406	438	469	500	531	563	594	625
35 mpg	257	286	314	343	371	400	429	457	486	514	543	571
40 mpg	225	250	275	300	325	350	375	400	425	450	475	500

*For a car that travels 15,000 miles a year, multiply the above figure by 1.5; for 7,500 miles, multiply by .75; and so forth. So, a 18 mpg car would cost $834 for 15,000 miles at $1.00 a gallon; and $417 for gas at 7,500 miles.

Table 12.2 Gas Mileage & Annual Fuel Costs (10,000 miles at $1 per gallon)

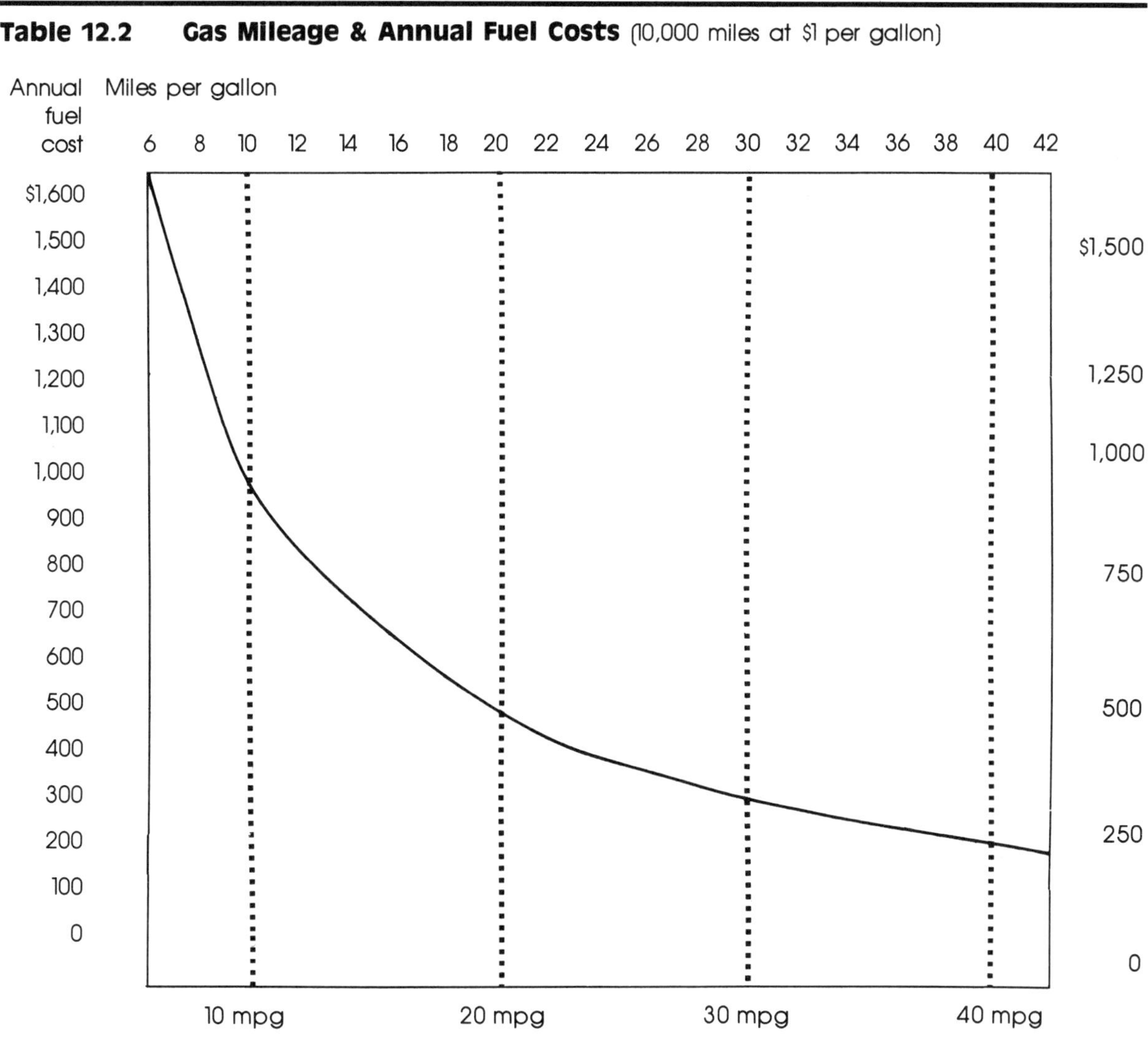

Table 12.3 Short Trips and Gas Mileage*

Number of trips on 25 gallons of gas	*Total miles possible*	*Gas mileage*	*Cost per mile (at $1 a gallon)*
Ten 40-mile trips	400	16.0 mpg	6.3¢
Sixty 4-mile trips	240	9.6 mpg	10.4¢
Ninety 2-mile trips	180	7.2 mpg	13.9¢
One hundred 1-mile trips	100	4.0 mpg	25.0¢

*Based on a study of the results of a test of a "typical family car," reported in the federal Environmental Agency's October 1976 pamphlet entitled "Factors Affecting Automotive Fuel Economy."

Table 12.4 Annual Fuel Cost Differences with Cheaper Gas (10,000 miles*)

Gas Mileage	Differences in price per gallon								
	1¢	2¢	3¢	4¢	5¢	6¢	7¢	8¢	9¢
8 mpg	$13	25	38	50	63	75	88	100	113
10 mpg	10	20	30	40	50	60	70	80	90
12 mpg	8	17	25	33	42	50	58	67	75
14 mpg	7	14	21	29	36	43	50	57	64
16 mpg	6	13	19	25	31	38	44	50	56
18 mpg	6	11	17	22	28	33	39	44	50
20 mpg	5	10	15	20	25	30	35	40	45
22 mpg	5	9	14	18	23	27	32	36	41
24 mpg	4	8	12	17	21	25	29	33	37
26 mpg	4	8	12	15	19	23	27	31	35
30 mpg	3	7	10	13	17	20	23	27	30
32 mpg	3	6	9	13	16	19	22	25	28
35 mpg	3	6	9	11	14	17	20	23	26
40 mpg	3	5	8	10	13	15	18	20	23

*As with Table 12.1, multiply the above figure by 0.5 to obtain the annual fuel cost difference for a car that travels 5,000 miles; 0.6 for 6,000 miles; .75 for 7,500 miles; 1.25 for 12,500 miles; and so forth. So, a 5¢ per gallon difference for a 18 mpg car for 12,500 miles is $35; and for 6,000 miles, $17 (rounded off to the nearest dollar).

13 UNLOADING your used car

You are now confronted with an ethical dilemma if you have carefully read the earlier chapters of this book. You not only know a lot more about the used car business than you did when you started the book, you also know considerably more than most nonprofessionals. You have an understanding of how the Blue Book works, how to haggle for a better price, and, most important, how some of the tricksters disguise problems with used cars.

With those bits of information you are in a good position to take advantage of an unsuspecting used car buyer. It's easy to make a quick buck in the used car trade, as any professional used car salesman will tell you.

I will leave the moral questions to you and your conscience and instead will devote this chapter to some practical advice about how to sell your used car. You certainly should not assume that you will automatically get the best of the deal selling your used car just because you understand the business better than most other people. Even the most experienced and talented used car hustlers occasionally "take a bath"—their phrase for losing money on a car.

What Not to Do

My friend Jennifer got an absolutely terrible deal when she sold her '72 Ford Pinto station wagon a few years ago. She had decided to move from California to New England several months earlier and planned to sell her car before she left town. Unfortunately for her pocketbook, she make no arrangements to sell the car before her last week in California, and the Pinto became another possession that she needed to dispose of quickly, sort of like her house plants.

Jennifer was already in the worst frame of mind to engage in used car bargaining. She was at the mercy of a potential buyer because she felt so rushed. Jennifer had bought the Pinto a year earlier from a new car dealer's used car lot for $2,000, and she wasn't about to leave her investment on the street for a city tow truck to cart off to the junk yard. Any deal was better than none, she thought.

A few days before her scheduled departure, Jennifer called up the closest new car dealership and asked whether they would be interested in buying her Pinto. The salesman (named Richard) expressed interest and suggested that she come to the lot where he could appraise the car. Rather than call other car lots, Jennifer drove to meet Richard.

At the lot Richard told Jennifer he wanted to examine the car before giving her a firm estimate. He walked around the Pinto very slowly and shook his head almost mournfully a few times. He seemed particularly engrossed while looking at the right front fender, which was slightly dented, and the side blinker light case, which had been removed. Richard touched his hand along a foot-long superficial scratch behind the front door and shook his head again. "It's real hard to do body work with these simulated wood panels," the salesman reported dourly.

The salesman then asked Jennifer to accompany him to his office where he plopped down in his chair and pulled out a little book that he said was the "Blue Book." He told Jennifer that although the Blue Book said the Pinto was worth "about $1,200," he would have to deduct some money for the broken right side light and the body work for the right fender and side of the car. He said that body work is really expensive, especially for cars with fake wood. "At the minimum, I'd have to subtract a couple hundred dollars," Richard told her.

Jennifer felt her heart sink as she realized that the man was saying that she might not be able to get even half of what she paid for the car only a year earlier. "Then, to give you a completely accurate appraisal, you would have to leave the car here so I could have one of the mechanics do a complete check of the engine, brakes, automatic transmission, and the like," the salesman continued. "Since it's Saturday, I couldn't give you an answer until Monday afternoon at the earliest. Judging from the appearance of the car, I'd say you might have a few things wrong with it mechanically. There always are problems, you know."

Consumer Auto Mart

Not all alternatives to the used car middleman succeed as well as Wheels & Deals (see photo, Chapter 1). In fact, some are monumental flops.

The entrepreneurs behind the Consumers Auto Mart planned to use the concept of a flea market and apply it to selling used cars. They rented the huge parking lot of the Oakland Coliseum (home of the Oakland Raiders and Oakland A's), and hoped for a huge turnout. Although several hundred car sellers brought their autos, few potential buyers showed up, possibly because of lack of publicity. The initiators of the mart decided they could not afford to pay the Coliseum's rental rates, so they halted the auto flea market after the first day.

By this time, Jennifer felt terribly disheartened. From the way the salesman was talking, she figured that she would meet the same problem at any other car dealer she visited. She was anxious to get rid of the car, and was willing to accept almost any reasonable offer.

Perhaps sensing her state of mind, the salesman suddenly said that he would be willing to forego the "usual expert mechanical appraisal." He said, "Look, I'd be willing to write out a check today for $875 for your car. That isn't really the way we normally do things here. But because you seem like such a nice girl, I'm willing to take your word that there's nothing seriously wrong with your Pinto's engine."

Jennifer accepted the offer immediately, though she had a feeling the salesman was getting a bargain. She just didn't understand how the car could have been worth $2,000 a year earlier, but only $875 then.

Several weeks after Jennifer left, I happened to notice her Pinto parked on a street. When I looked closely, I noticed that the right front side light had been replaced but the dent and scratch were still apparent. Subsequently, I double checked the salesman's quote from the Blue Book. I saw that at the time she sold the car, a '72 Pinto station wagon had a retail (high Blue Book) value of $1,870 and a wholesale (low Blue Book) value of $1,225. That accounts for the "about $1,200" the salesman talked about. But when I looked at the Blue Book more closely, I noticed that the simulated wood panel, which Ford calls the "Squire option," is worth another $150. That meant the Pinto's actual wholesale Blue Book price was $1,375, which is nearly $200 more than the salesman quoted to my friend.

I presume that what happened was that the dealer paid Jennifer the $875, put about $25 maximum into fixing the right front side light, and spent another $35 or so to have the car detailed (washed, waxed, the engine steamcleaned, and so on). Even if the dealer spent another $50 on the car, he still would have invested less than $1,000 in a nice-looking and well-running automobile. I will never know what the Pinto's next owner paid for the car. But it's safe to assume that it would have been close to the going Blue Book retail price of the car – $1,870.

What is most disturbing is that had Jennifer spent a little extra time, known the actual Blue Book price of her car, and taken her car to a few dealers to get other estimates, she undoubtedly could have received an additional $200 to $300 for the car.

I think now that she could have easily received between $300 and $600 more than the $875 if she had sold the car to a private party, rather than a used car salesman. Instead, the car dealer pocketed close to a thousand dollars for a few minutes' work.

Selling to a Dealer or to a Private Party

You can almost always get a higher price for your used car from a private party than from a dealer. Aside from the obvious point that a professional used car salesman can normally outhaggle an amateur, the Blue Book makes it advantageous to avoid dealers. Jennifer's experience was typical. If you are selling a used car, many dealers use the Blue Book's wholesale value of your car as the maximum they will offer you, while they often deduct from that price for any flaws they spot.

By contrast, a private party wanting to buy a used car from you is often interested in buying a car for less than what a dealer would typically demand (the retail or high Blue Book value). But most private party buyers also would be willing to settle for a price that is substantially higher than what you would get by selling it to a dealer (the wholesale or low Blue Book value). Again, as has been shown in earlier chapters, the best way to beat the used car hustle is to use the Blue Book to *your* advantage.

You should sell your car privately even if you plan to buy a new car. Don't be misled by the great trade-in offers advertised by new car dealers. Although a new car salesman tells you he will give you more for your used car on a trade-in than its Blue Book (wholesale) value, he usually will mark up the difference by charging you more for the new car.

When trading in your car for a new one or another used car, pay attention to the *difference* between what the salesman says your car is worth and the price of the new car. That difference – which equals the amount you would have to pay for the newer car – is the only relevant figure to keep in mind when comparing the deal offered by one dealer versus another dealer.

Many dealers go so far as to keep two sets of books to handle trade-in deals, according to several car salesmen I have interviewed. Here's how it works. Let's say you're interested in buying a new car with a sticker price of $5,000. The salesman may tell you that he'll give you $2,000 for your used car as a trade-in even though its Blue Book value is only $1,750, and he may also knock off another $100 from the sticker price, so that you think you are buying the car for only an extra $2,900. At this point, you think you have saved yourself $250 on the price of your new car. What the salesman doesn't tell you is that although he will write up your sales slip to reflect a trade-in value of $2,000 for your car, the dealer writes in his own records that he sold the new car for $4,750 with a $1,750 trade-in.

There are endless variations of tricks car dealers can play when it comes to juggling trade-in prices, sticker prices, Blue Book prices, and so forth. Suffice it to say that they know what they are doing and that they usually come out ahead on any bargain – way ahead.

What you should keep in mind in considering trading in a used car for a new one or another used one is that car salesmen would generally prefer not having to hassle with used cars which often become liabilities for the dealer. With very few exceptions, they feel they are better off with what they call a "clean deal," one without a trade-in. Consequently, a customer willing to pay cash for a new car gets a better deal in terms of dollars and cents than one who brings a trade-in into the bargain.

What I have outlined about new car trade-in deals goes double for selling cars older than six or seven years, even when you are not trying to buy another car from a dealer. Older cars are hard for them to sell. Most new car dealers simply do not retail older vehicles, so they have to sell them to auto wholesalers or used car lots, often for an extremely low price, such as $200. By the same token, a used car dealer won't be interested in buying your older used car for a higher price when he can get a similar older car from a new car dealer at a cheap wholesale price.

In short, only private individuals interested in safe, reliable transportation pay a reasonable price for older used cars that offer what they're looking for. That's why any clunker monger and most third-handers should avoid dealers altogether, when selling their used cars.

To sum up: YOU SHOULD ONLY SELL A USED CAR TO A DEALER IF YOU HAVE NEITHER THE TIME NOR THE ENERGY TO SELL IT YOURSELF.

Preparing Your Car for Sale

Whether you plan to sell your car privately or to a dealer, you can take several steps to make it easier to sell, and possibly earn you extra dollars.

1. Paperwork Make sure you have all the official papers ready for the sale, such as registration and title. At the same time, you should assemble all your receipts for major repairs and/or parts (tires, battery, and so on). This may be important evidence to a potential buyer that you have maintained the car properly.

2. Mechanical Repairs You can take one of two routes: Sell the car in its present condition and inform the buyer of needed repairs, or fix all or most of the mechanical defects and hope to pass the expense on to the buyer.

The first alternative may seem especially attractive if your car is facing a major repair job, such as an engine overhaul or transmission work. Make sure you know what is wrong with the car before you decide to take this course since what you consider to be a major problem may merely be a minor repair bill. For instance, you may think that the loud missing noise you hear in the engine means something terrible has gone wrong with the car, whereas a simple mechanical diagnosis would reveal that one of the spark plug wires is loose.

If you decide to make some mechanical repairs before selling the car, you should concentrate on the ones that increase the value of the car the most and do not cost very much. For instance, many car buyers would pass up a car with poor brakes. Unless your car's entire brake system is shot, you should be able to have the brakes working and in top shape for less than $100. When you advertise the car, you can also make a big point about the fact that it has new brakes, which makes it much more valuable to the buyer than a similar car with poor brakes.

3. Detailing Take a tip from the professional car sellers. Make the car look nice before you attempt to put it on the market. You can do car "detail" or "manicure" work yourself — wash and wax the car, vacuum the interior and trunk. Or you can take the car to a professional car wash and wax business where they will do that work for you for $5 to $10.

If you are selling a car worth more than about $1,500 or $2,000, you may want to have the car cleaned and fixed up by a professional auto detailer. (They should be listed under "Automobile Detailing" in your phone book's Yellow Pages. Also, many garage mechanics and body shop workers know of other freelance auto detailers.) For $50 to $100, these professionals can make your car look great — or at least as good as can be expected. You may not even recognize the car after they finish with it. (One used car salesman told me some detailers even have what's called "new car smell," which they can put in a car to give it the odor of a brand new vehicle.)

Just keep in mind that professional used car salesmen routinely have their cars detailed for a good reason. It's a wise investment that invariably pays for itself many times over.

One of the recent Federal Trade Commission studies underscored this point. In the previously cited National Analysts survey of 400 used car buyers, 97 percent rated the "car's overall mechanical condition" as an "important or very important" factor in their decision to buy the car, and 95 percent gave the same response to a "car's general physical appearance." These two factors — its mechanical condition and appearance — were rated much higher than any of the other factors, such as the car's mileage, make, model, or body style. Even more significantly, nearly half of the people interviewed (49.6 percent) said they assumed that cars that had a good physical appearance would also be in good mechanical condition.

In other words, about half of the people think that a car that looks good runs well. Remember that point when you sell your car.

One final point: If your car has any dents or ugly scratches, you may find it worthwhile to have them fixed in a body shop. But body work is a much trickier proposition than having your car detailed. Not only can this become extremely expensive, but you may not earn back your investment when you sell the car. It is similar to doing mechanical repairs before selling the car. You have to determine whether it is worth spending the extra money for body work on the basis of how extensive the repairs would be and how much they would cost. What's worse, body work does not bring a car back to its original shape or color.

4. Advertising One of the cheapest and most effective methods of advertising your car is to place a "For Sale" sign in the car window. When I sold my Datsun B-210, I received nearly as many phone calls from people who had seen my car on the street as from those who responded to my newspaper want-ad. (I wrote my phone number in large numbers beneath the "For Sale" sign. Some people also write brief descriptions of their car and their asking price on the car window.)

Make sure to write a full description of your vehicle if you insert a want-ad in a newspaper classified section. At the very minimum, you should state your asking price. You may save yourself some unnecessary calls if you also include whether the car is a two-door, four-door, or station wagon; has automatic or manual transmission; or possesses distinctive features, such as an FM radio, tape deck, air conditioning, or new equipment like new brakes or new tires. (See want-ad jargon glossary, Table 13.1.)

If you have also detailed the car, make sure to state that the car is "clean" or some similar phrase. Don't oversell the car in your want-ad, but you shouldn't feel reluctant to use an extra line of ad space to describe your car's finer features. If your car is on its last mechanical legs, however, you should state that it needs repair work in your ad. That, too, will prevent unwanted phone calls.

When you sell the car privately, you should be prepared to engage in some

Haggling

When you seel the car privately, you should be prepared to engage in some bargaining. The general principles are similar to those for someone buying a used car, as outlined in Chapter 9.

To reemphasize a few points about haggling that are especially applicable to a seller, here are three items to keep in mind:

Know your minimum. Decide in advance what you want for the car. You should ask for a little more when you advertise the car, such as in a newspaper ad, in order to give yourself some room to move when you bargain with a potential buyer. But do not bargain below the minimum you want for the car.

Know your car's market value. As with buying a car, you should make an attempt to learn your car's Blue Book value. When you begin to bargain with a prospective buyer, you should start with the high Blue Book (retail) value of the car. You may even start higher if you think your car is in better shape than average or has extra options such as a tape deck and air conditioning. You can point out that the Blue Book states that your price is what the car normally retails for. (Again, if the buyer does not understand the difference between retail and wholesale values, you may feel that it would be discrete to keep that information to yourself.)

If you are selling an older car not listed in the Blue Book, you should comb the newspaper want-ads to determine the approximate value of the car on the local used car market.

Be willing to refuse final offers. As with buying a car, your ability to say "no" is your ultimate bargaining tool. If a potential buyer is offering less than you think the car is worth, refuse the offer. You might tell them that you have been hoping to get more. If their offer is the best you receive, you could get their phone number and call them back to see if they are still interested.

Again, as with everything related to buying and selling used cars, PATIENCE is the trait you should cultivate when you attempt to unload your used car.

Table 13.1 An Auto Want-Ad Glossary

Abbreviation	Meaning
ac, a.c., a/c, AC, air	air conditioning
as is	being sold in its present condition
at, auto	automatic transmission
bat	battery
bo, best	best offer
brks	brakes
4 cyl, 6 cyl	four-cylinder or six-cylinder engine
cu	cubic inch, as 307 cu means 307-cubic-inch engine
dlr	dealer
2 dr, 4 dr	two door or four door
e/c, ex cnd	excellent condition
4 whd	four wheel drive
k	thousand miles, as 43k means 43,000 miles
lo mi	low mileage
man	manual transmission
mech spec	mechanic's special, in poor mechanical shape
nds wk	needs work
pb	power brakes
pnt	paint
ps	power steering
pu	pick up truck
pwr ant	power antenna
rads, rdls	radial tires
r.b., rblt	rebuilt
r&h	radio and heater
snrf	sunroof
3 spd, 4 spd	three-speed or four-speed manual transmission
stick, std	manual or standard transmission
tran, trans	transmission
wgn	station wagon
ww	whitewall tires